D1301744

the BIG book

of FAMILY FUN

the BIG book of FAMILY FUN

GWEN ELLIS

GRAMERCY BOOKS
NEW YORK

Scripture marked RSV is taken from the Revised Standard Version of the Bible, copyright 1946, 1952, 1971 by the Division of Christian Education of the National Council of the Churches of Chr in the USA. Used by permission.

Scripture marked KJV is taken from the King James Version of the Bible.

Scripture marked Phillips is taken from The New Testament in Modern English. © 1958, 1960, 1972 by J. B. Phillips and published by The Macmillan Company.

This 2001 edition is published by Gramercy Books™,
an imprint of Random House Value Publishing, Inc.,
280 Park Avenue, New York, New York 10017,
by arrangement with Baker Book House Company.

Gramercy Books™ and design are trademarks of Random House Value Publishing, Inc.

Random House
New York • Toronto • London • Sydney • Auckland
http://www.randomhouse.com/

Printed and bound in the United States of America

Library of Congress Cataloging-in-Publication Data

Ellis, Gwen, 1938–
    The big book of family fun / Gwen Ellis.
        p. cm.
    Originally published: Grand Rapids, Mich. : Fleming H. Revell, c1999.
    Includes bibliographical references.
    ISBN 0-517-16355-1
  1. Parenting—United States. 2. Parents—Time management—United States. 3. Family recreation—United States. 4. Child rearing—United States. I. Title.

HQ755.8 .E38 2001
649'.1—dc21

00-067270

8 7 6 5 4 3 2 1

Contents

Part 3 ✳ Finding Dollars for Family Fun

Preface

You think it will last forever—your children's childhood. You think you will always be dealing with diapers, orthodontists, school conferences, and skinned knees. But you won't. Soon you'll find yourself walking past the infants' section of a large department store, then the toddlers' department, and before you know it, you'll be shopping in the children's department. I began to realize when I'd walked past all of those sections and even passed the teen department (because I couldn't choose anything my teens would wear) that childhood is really very short. And that's why we need to make the most of it—why we have to get rid of the "we'll-do-it-someday" mentality.

This book is a compilation of three books I wrote, attempting to share the adventure, excitement, and joy I experienced raising my two children. They tell me now that they had a wonderful childhood and I find great satisfaction in that fact.

I've packed this volume with every idea I could think of about having fun as a family, managing your time so that you can have fun, and saving money so that you have some left for family activities. I've tried to point up the importance of investing both time and money in your children while you have them at home. And as a true believer in goal setting, I've showed you plans and ideas for deciding what's truly important to your family.

I hope and pray that you will find this volume something you turn to again and again while your children are growing up. I hope it becomes a book you pass on to your children after they marry and start their families because the principles and ideas contained here are timeless. These are the bedrock on which to build a great childhood for your children.

Part 1

Ideas for Family Fun

I'm glad I learned to play and I'm especially glad I learned to play with my children. When I think of the places we've been and the experiences we've shared together, my memories are very sweet. There are innumerable things families can do together, such as walking ocean beaches, camping on the top of mountains and in valleys, walking in the rain, visiting zoos and game farms and seeing bears, moose, deer, elk, beaver, mountain goats, game birds, otters, whales, trout, bald eagles, pikes, groundhogs, and hundreds of others of God's creatures.

You don't have to know very much to play with a child. The child is an expert at play; she'll teach *you*. Give any child some sunshine, water, and time, and she can amuse herself for hours. She will be happiest if you are there too, helping her dam up the stream, laughing, talking, planning how to build the dam even bigger, and then plotting how you're going to "crash it down."

Play doesn't have to be elaborate or complicated. What the child wants is you and your undivided attention. She wants you to be there, not only your body, but also your eyes, your heart, and yourself. You may fool some people into thinking you are paying attention to them but you can't fool your child.

As you spend time playing and talking with your children, you will have opportunities to find out what they're thinking, what false values they're picking up from their friends, and what problems they're encountering in their world. Some children don't share easily and need extended time with a parent before they're ready to open up and confide their deepest thoughts.

Playtime is also a time to teach spiritual lessons. Values and priorities can be taught best in the course of everyday living, and wise parents learn to take advantage of every opportunity. As parents spend time with their children and look for openings for talk, they will be able to teach about God's goodness, his provision, and the difference between right and wrong. When this is done in the course of everyday life, the child learns in a natural, open way. She never feels as though she's getting a sermon.

Family fun rarely comes looking for you. You have to determine to get out there and discover it with your children. It's not going to happen unless you set aside some time, plan where to go and what to do, and then get up and get going.

You don't have to know very much to play with a child.

Family Fun Essentials

1

Planning

Planning Is Vital

Planning is a vital part of teaching our children our values through shared experiences. We have to plan to spend time with them. We have to plan the time we spend with them. And we have to plan what values we want them to acquire through the experience. If we fail to plan, other commitments will swallow the time we should be giving to our family.

Making no plan is a plan in itself—a plan to fail at spending time with the most important people on earth, our family. Busy fathers and mothers must write "special appointment" across an evening, a day, or a week and then keep that special appointment as if it were a sacred obligation. It is. I can assure you that twenty years from now you will not remember what other things you *could have done* on those evenings given to your family, but none of you will ever forget what you *did*.

Planning for shared adventures begins to falter when no one in the family takes it on as a special assignment. Someone who enjoys the task should be responsible for doing it. If no one in your family enjoys planning, you can make the planning itself a family event. Remember that planning takes time. This means that the individual or the family doing the planning must block out another segment of time for planning. Take an evening or a weekend afternoon and make a tentative plan for the next six months. Get a calendar and start filling in dates with family activities.

Much can be learned from the give-and-take involved as family members discuss their ideas and wishes about having fun. Probably the first thing learned is that somebody has to give in to the ideas of others, at least some of the time. Before your planning session it would be wise to lay some ground rules such as: Nobody calls anybody else's idea stupid; and everybody has to suggest at least one idea sometime during the evening.

Coming Up with Ideas

Where *does* one find ideas about activities to do as a family? I know this is a problem because parents often ask me where they can hike that won't be too strenuous for a five-year-old child, or what inexpensive event could nine- to twelve-year-old children do for a birthday party. And usually I have an idea to share or I can look in my files for further suggestions. (More about files in a minute.)

One source of information about local activities is the library. Most libraries are filled with regional publications: books, pamphlets, maps, and much more material. Ask your librarian to show you the regional section and write down those things that catch your attention.

One source of information about local activities is the library.

Another helpful section in the library is the travel section. If your planning will take you beyond your region, you should spend time investigating this section. There you will find books with travel ideas for all budgets—from backpacking to the most elegant hotels and restaurants.

Often the library has a stack of pamphlets and folders about current events in your city. Ask to see these. The library itself may have a full schedule of events such as puppet shows, movies, story hours, and special guests. Get a printed schedule of these events.

Visit the local chamber of commerce. It too will have a list of local and regional events, and who knows what else you may find? Most people never fully explore their own neighborhoods, cities, counties, and regions. There is probably more to do within a ten-mile radius of your home than you could accomplish in a month of leisure time.

Use the Internet for information on a vast array of subjects. You can find Web sites for places you'd like to visit or for every conceivable activity you may want to pursue, from hang gliding to stamp collecting.

Bookstores are treasure troves of information and ideas. Spend an afternoon browsing the shelves with your kids. Again, focus on the regional publications and travel books. Buy a few; they are a choice investment in your family's future. These books will give you ideas of places to go and help you understand the historical background of the places you will visit. Incidentally, you are not only gathering information about places to go and things to do, but you are also teaching your children the value of books and how to find information on a given topic.

Regional magazines are an excellent source of information about places to see and things to do in your area. Most Sunday papers have a magazine section containing local activities and interests. The travel section of the newspaper has information about upcoming events in your city. Our local weekend paper has a "What's Up?" section listing everything from area garage sales to dog shows. Many national magazines have a regional section brimming with all kinds of interesting information.

What about the yellow pages? Our phone book lists dozens and dozens of travel agencies, and all of them have someone sitting at the other end of a phone line just waiting for your call. They can help you with travel plans—from taking a Greyhound bus to a nearby city to flying to Europe.

Don't overlook another important source—your friends and acquaintances. Make it a practice to ask people what they like to do when they have some free time. Where do they like to go? What is their favorite restaurant in your area and why do they enjoy it so much? Ask them about their favorite free activities in your area.

Every time you ask friends for their ideas, you will probably learn something you didn't know. The people with the best ideas are those who enjoy doing things—those who don't mind putting forth some effort to be active. Don't expect good ideas from people who spend their Saturdays watching television.

Organizing Ideas

Enough adventure ideas to fill a book have probably already passed through your hands. You may have read an article in the newspaper about a place you would like to see, but instead of taking action, you folded the paper, laid it down, and forgot all about it.

The best way to organize newspaper and magazine clippings is in a file. A filing system doesn't have to be elaborate, but it is essential to have some system for keeping track of information. All you need are some file folders and a cardboard box to hold them.

I have about 150 file folders labeled with places to go and things to see. Let's pick one at random and see what's in it. How about "Florida"? Hmmm. The file contains a lot of information I brought home from my last business trip to Florida. There's airline information, pamphlets about St. Augustine, Vizcaya, and the Keys. Here's a pamphlet about a London Fog coat outlet in Florida. And here's some more information about outlet centers.

Check out the Internet, bookstores, regional magazines, and the Yellow Pages.

Here's an article clipped from *USA Today:* "Orlando Unlimited: Fun Doesn't Stop with Disney." It lists eleven attractions in addition to Walt Disney World. The file contains more about central Florida. Did you know you can take a sunrise balloon ride over Cinderella's Castle and the surrounding area?

And here is an article suggesting what to do when your money runs out—visit the Tupperware World Headquarters. The last pieces in this file folder are two *Southern Living* magazine articles about Florida and a clipping that lists an 800 number to call for help with reservations.

I think after looking into this folder, we're about ready for a trip to Florida.

The secret to having plenty of information when you pursue an adventure is to gather that information in advance. Write for free travel information, or let your kids clip and mail the travel coupons in magazines. They'll be helping you and they'll enjoy receiving the information in the mail. Your problem will be getting them to part with the brochures so you can file them.

Train yourself to watch for ideas and then clip them out on the spot. Probably someone will complain about the hole in the newspaper or magazine, but that someone will forgive you when you have just the right information at the moment it is needed in the future.

There are several methods for filing information. You can file by location or by family interests. Filing by location is easy to understand, but let me explain how to file by interests.

Watch for information on your family's special interest. If your family is interested in antique cars, start collecting information about antique car shows and displays. Put all that information together in the same file folder, regardless of the geographic location. If your family loves ice cream, watch for information about ice cream. Tear it out and file it in your "Ice Cream" folder. Then when you have a yen to go someplace unusual for ice cream, you can pull out the information you need.

Another way to file information is by subject. Here are some possible headings to start you thinking about your file:

 Agriculture

Dairy farms: Most will give a tour if you call ahead.

Farms: Pick your own fruit and vegetables. Watch for ads and roadside signs.

Horse ranches: Visit the blacksmith shop.

Research farms: You may learn of the latest discoveries.

 Arts

Ballet: Expose your children to ballet. *The Nutcracker* is a delightful story and is performed annually in many cities.

Opera: This can be fun for the whole family—if it is sung in English and if everyone knows the story before the singing begins.

Art galleries: Visit permanent exhibits and keep watch for changing exhibits.

Communications

TV stations: Watch for times when stations are open for visits.

Radio stations: Let your children see the announcers and disc jockeys they hear on the air.

Telephone companies: Tour a facility and learn about modern communication systems.

 Cultural

Folk festivals: These are plentiful in most states throughout the summer months.

Ethnic food fairs: Make the rounds. Watch for announcements in the newspaper and on television.

Native American events: You'll find these in many states, not just in the West.

 Drama

Seasonal events: In our area *A Christmas Carol* is performed annually.

Theatrical performances in city parks: Check the newspaper.

Community theaters: Some may be children's theater.

 Government

Government buildings: Many have tours.

Courts of law: These are interesting places to visit and in most cases can be viewed when court is not in session.

Police stations and fire stations: Call to find out their schedules for tours.

 History

Sunday paper: History seems to be a favorite topic for newspaper writers. Clip interesting articles and save.

State parks: Write to your state park system for information. They are often built on historical sites.

Old homes and buildings: Tours are offered annually by many societies. Watch for the announcements in the newspapers.

Regional publications: Sunset in the West and *Southern Living* in the South often include information about historical events and places. Read the library issues and photocopy the articles that interest you.

 Industry

Candy factories: Guests are usually welcome. You'll have to make arrangements to tour the larger ones. Most have a seconds (rejects) shop that will make them a favorite stop for your family.

Pulp mills: See how paper is made.

Woolen and cotton mills: Learn about making fabrics.

Other factories in your area

 Nature

Botany: File information on formal gardens and arboretums where you can see regional plants.

Marine life: If you live near the ocean or a lake, this may be of interest.

Wild animals: Keep information on zoos and game farms.

Birds: Some people make a lifelong hobby of watching birds.

Astronomy: Locate planetariums worth visiting.

 Science

Science centers and museums: There are many events geared for children and young people.

Universities: Science programs through the year are often open to the public. Call their offices, make notes of their programs, and file them.

 Transportation

Trains: Collect schedules to the nearest towns. If your children have never ridden on a train, plan to do it.

Model trains: In our area we have two very fine clubs that love to have visitors. It's amazing to see the amount of time and energy grown men put into playing with trains!

Airplanes: Airports and air museums are fascinating places for kids.

Trucks: Visit a local dispatcher or a truck terminal and watch how truckers handle the big rigs. Maybe you'll be able to ride in a cab of a truck.

Mapping Out the Plan

Let's suppose you found something of interest in your file—an adventure you want to pursue. Now it is time to plan the event. The following checklist will help you:

1. Who's going on this adventure? Mom? Dad? Dad and one child? Mom and a child?
2. How far away is it?
3. What time do you need to leave?
4. What kind of clothing is appropriate?
5. Do you need to take a lunch?
6. How much money will you need?
7. Is there enough gas in the car?
8. If it is a ticketed event, have you bought the tickets?
9. Where are the tickets?
10. How long will you be gone?
11. Will you need to eat a meal on the road or in a restaurant?
12. What will you do in the car on the way?
13. What favorite toy, blanket, or pillow should be taken so there are no tears later because it is missing?
14. Have you done some background reading? Don't forget the book so that you can share what you've learned on the way or when you arrive.

The checklist is completed. You're ready to launch.

When Plans Go Wrong

Not all plans work out as expected. The best plans do go awry sometimes. You can't do much about that, except possibly to have an alternative plan. It may not be your first choice and may not be quite as exciting, but having an alternative plan will help take the sting out of losing the first adventure. Some of our most memorable adventures began when a prior plan failed. Be prepared to regroup and head in another direction.

I've said it before, but it bears repeating: We can't teach our children our values unless we spend quality time with them, and quality time must be planned. Block out time on the calendar, gather the information, do the research so that you know what to expect, file research information where you can find it, and bring your children into your planning process. If the plan fails, regroup and do something else.

If we take the time to plan our adventures carefully, we will reap the full benefit of shared experience with our children, and they will learn what we treasure and value in our lives.

Curiosity

All of childhood is a time of curiosity, but the peak time of curiosity is the period between ages three and five. If you don't have one in your own household, borrow a three-year-old child for the afternoon. Follow him around and watch him. He will feel things, poke his finger into things, lick things, jump on and off things, pull on things, and if you leave him alone long enough, he will produce absolute chaos.

He will ask questions and more questions. Research shows that three-year-old children ask more than three hundred questions a day. They ask questions for many reasons. They ask to gather information: "What's that?" they'll ask, pointing to a dog. They ask to try to deal with some underlying fear: "Will you still be my mommy when I'm grown up?" They ask to try to separate the real world from fantasy: "Did King Kong really live?" And they ask questions to practice asking questions and answering them themselves: "Where are you going today? I know, you're going shopping."

Encourage It

Create an atmosphere where questions are allowed and encouraged. Research shows that curious, questioning children are better equipped emotionally and intellectually than the less curious. They do better in school, are generally quicker at solving problems, and are more flexible and creative.

Children are naturally curious, so encouraging their curiosity isn't difficult. Think about the infant who is learning to crawl. Mother is continually taking strange things out of the crawler's mouth. But it is through his mouth that he learns about hardness and softness, cold and heat, wet and dry. Everything goes into the mouth because that is how he satisfies his curiosity about an object—at least for a while.

No matter what the child's age—infant, toddler, elementary-school age or older—parents need to encourage, not stifle, curiosity. By allowing and encouraging curiosity, you grow creative people; curiosity is the seedbed of creativity.

Provide children with tactile, sensory experiences that allow their curiosity to flourish.

Stimulate It

Let's return to the three-year-old child. He's as curious as he can be. You can spend the day taking things out of his hands, pulling him down from places he doesn't belong, or—as we once had to do because our attention shifted for a moment and one of our children decided to taste paint thinner—making a quick dash to the emergency room.

Instead of spending all your time saying no or don't, provide children with tactile, sensory experiences that allow their curiosity to flourish. Regardless of the age of children, we need to provide them with an environment that stimulates their curiosity.

Let them play in the cookie or bread dough. They're dying to know what it feels like. And why don't you get in there and squeeze the dough through your fingers with them? Let them hold a newborn chick, and then you take your turn. Rub its soft down on your cheek and watch your children's eyes when you do. Let them smell the earthy scent of mushrooms, the tang of lemon peel, and the never-to-be-forgotten aroma of candy canes.

Provide them with blunt scissors and an old catalog so they can cut out the pictures. Let them splash in water and blow soap bubbles. Take your child to a hillside and blow the biggest bubbles ever seen. (If you add a little glycerin to the soapy water, it makes stronger bubbles. Use a huge ring, like a rounded-out coat hanger, to make bubbles. The really big rings make really big bubbles. The record is twenty-four feet across.) The children will learn all kinds of wonderful things from these experiences, and so will you. And all of you will have shared in the adventure of curiosity.

Maybe your children are no longer toddlers, but are in school. And maybe you have never considered using curiosity as a tool for family adventure. I suggest that you take a half-hour walk together and agree that you will ask questions about everything you see. Take a pad and pencil to record what is spotted. Then promise each other that you will learn the answers to your curiosity questions.

2

Treasures in Your Own Home

Family Night

Family night is one of the ways to maximize the influence of parents and home on children. It's not a new idea. In fact family night has been around for many years. But even though it is not new, it's an important idea—perhaps more important now than ever before because of our increasingly busy lifestyle.

What can a family do that everyone will enjoy? How do you get beyond the complaints that "this is boring"? The possibilities are limitless. But first, you'll need some rules. Let the kids make the rules; they'll be more likely to keep them if they do. You will have to keep referring to them, probably as long as you have a family night at your house. You may also have to revise them from time to time.

Here are some suggestions:

1. We will keep one night a week for family night. This need not be the same night every week. We'll try to plan far enough ahead so that everyone can clear his or her calendar and be there.
2. Each family member will take turns planning the programs for the evening. No one gets out of taking his or her turn. If

one family member is very busy that week, she can switch with another family member, but she must take her turn later.

3. No complaining or fidgeting. No statements like, "This is dumb," or "I could have done this better." Remember, you'll get your chance to prove how good you are as we take turns planning family night events.

4. Everyone will participate and cooperate, even when the planning is done by the youngest member of the family, and may seem too elementary to the oldest. (It's Mom and Dad's job to protect the self-esteem of the younger children in the home. Permanent damage can be done to fragile egos when older children are allowed to belittle younger ones in a family.)

In this first rule-setting, planning time, it is also important to talk about the purpose of family night. Communicate to each other why a family needs to get together on a regular basis. This is a great time to talk about the value of family loyalty, sharing, commitment, and togetherness.

Two purposes I would like to suggest are:

1. *To have fun together as a family.* Family night should be the most looked-forward-to night of the week. It should carry a sense of surprise and adventure. It can and should be a time of great anticipation.

2. *To worship the Lord together.* For Christian parents, a prime purpose for family night is to mold your children into strong, committed Christians, able to stand in an increasingly secular society. Family night is a time when children can watch their parents model devotion to and worship of God.

Decide as far ahead as possible which night will be family night each week. Scheduling the same night every week will simplify your life. We couldn't do that, and so used a different night each week.

As far ahead as possible, plan who will be in charge on a particular night. Post a schedule, and someone will have to help the younger ones remember their night. They will be learning the value of accepting responsibility and following through on an assignment.

Assign a night to each family member. That person can plan anything she wants. She will have to decide whether she can handle it alone, or if she needs Dad to drive the car somewhere or Mom to purchase some special supplies for the event. The more the child can do on her own, the more she will learn about planning and carrying out a plan.

Scripture reading and a prayer time should be part of the family night plan. Once again, younger children may need some help, but let them go as far as they can on their own. What they need most is encouragement. The Scripture can be from a favorite storybook or from an easy-to-read Bible. The prayer can be one or two sentences from each member of the family. God isn't concerned about the complexity or finesse of the prayer and Bible reading, and we shouldn't be either.

Suggested Family Night Events

Here are some ideas to get you started thinking about your family night:

Concern Night. Plan a family project to help someone like a missionary, elderly person, shut-in, relative, or someone who needs encouragement.

I remember the fun we had putting together a survival kit for a young woman who moved from Seattle to my small hometown in Montana. This was an unheard-of event. People leave that little town in droves to seek their fame and fortune in the big cities around the country. No one ever moves from a big city to that mountain village.

My children often had visited their grandparents, who still live there, and they knew what it would be like for this young woman to exchange neon marquees for two stoplights hanging in the middle of Main Street. They knew that rapid transit there often means a four-wheel rig, not a high-speed train.

I don't remember all the things that went into that survival kit but I do remember that the children insisted on including mosquito repellent and insect bite ointment. They had often been victims of the whining, bloodsucking hordes of mosquitoes that drive man and beast to distraction during the early summer in Montana.

We probably included a book or two for the long, slow evenings. There may have been fishhooks since the town's common philosophy is that "God doesn't take away from a man's life the hours he spends fishing."

We plotted, planned, laughed, and laughed some more as we packed the box. I remember the children ran all over the house gathering things to tuck inside. It was a lot of fun.

Celebration Night. Plan a party to honor someone in the family on a special occasion (like a good report card) or plan a party to celebrate some special day (like St. Patrick's Day). In a later chapter I'll give you more ideas about celebrating special days.

Fun Night. Plan an evening of fun and games at home. I have to confess that I hate table games, and whenever possible, I squirm my way out of them. When table games were the main event of the evening, I had to check my attitude and remember our participation rule. Usually it ended up being more fun than I had expected.

Outing Night. Plan some kind of adventure away from home. It could be a trip to an observatory or an evening at the circus.

On one outing night we took advantage of a very special Christmas event in our area. All of the boat owners decorate their boats with lights and play Christmas music. Everyone on board ship dresses in Christmas costumes, and then they parade their boats from one lake to another through a body of water known as the Montlake Cut.

For years a family in our church has lived on a houseboat floating in the Montlake Cut. One year they invited us to their home to watch the Christmas ships. We bundled up in coats and scarves, stood on their houseboat deck, drank hot cider, and watched the ships sail by. It was a very special evening.

Media Night. Plan and give a media presentation using slides, filmstrips, homemade videos, cartoon strips, and other visual aids.

Project Night. Provide materials for the family to make a project—art, drama, a table game, handicraft, or anything that comes to mind.

At our house the project often was a puppet show. We accumulated an impressive selection of puppets over the years. Some were gifts from relatives, some I found in thrift shops, and some I made. Some of our favorites were puppets made from paper bags or socks. It wasn't the artistic quality of the puppets that mattered, but the fun of making and using them.

Sometimes a Bible story looked quite strange when Daniel was played by a dog puppet and Esther by a sock puppet, but where the visual image failed, the kids' imaginations soared. It just didn't matter how true to life the puppets were.

A puppet theater need be no more than a large cardboard box with a hole cut in it, set on a table, or you can forget the box and let the puppeteers operate from behind the sofa.

Drama Night. Drama was another fun event at our house, and we all got involved. I usually pulled the shades so we didn't have to explain to the neighbors why we were running around in our bathrobes and wearing crowns on our heads.

I used to have a huge, old-fashioned trunk that was stuffed with costumes, accumulated through years of dramatic presentations.

Puppet shows are a fun family project.

Often for our family dramas, we read a Bible story together and then decided how to dramatize it. Each family member chose or was assigned a part. Then he or she dug into the costume trunk for something appropriate to wear. We would act out the story, sometimes switching parts several times during the evening. Usually the kids wanted to do "just one more" drama.

Outreach Night. Discuss and plan with the family a way to influence some other family for Christ. This might be the most difficult family-night event of all. One way to influence another family for Christ is to pray for them. That isn't too difficult. It is a little harder to reach out to those people in some way. Yet as Christians, our purpose on earth is to reach the lost. We must continue to emphasize this value to our children on an ongoing basis.

One time we read the Great Commission (Matt. 28:18–20). We formed a prayer list for other families and then we discussed ways we could reach those people for Christ. We decided we could invite them to a special event at our church, ask them to our home for dinner, share something we have, or take them something—like a cake or a meal. As we did these things, we would look for an opportunity to share Christ with them.

Some of those people have not yet found the Lord, but some of the people we prayed for have become Christians. Most notable was a family of boys who lived a couple of houses away and spent their summers lobbing eggs onto our house and into our backyard. After a while the entire family found Christ, and their conversion brought peace to the neighborhood.

Bible Night. One way to do Bible night is for the person in charge to find a passage of Scripture that is meaningful to her and to come up with a fun way to discuss it together, or make it come alive through many of the avenues we have discussed— drama, media, project, and so on.

A fun exercise is to read a Bible passage and then give magazines to family members. Let them tear out and glue onto a poster—collage fashion—pictures that illustrate the meaning of the Bible passage.

Talk-It-Over Night. Select a topic and write discussion questions. Then answer them together. This activity helps to develop your children into good conversationalists—people who can think for themselves and who can express their ideas well. Some children are more verbal than others, so watch that one or two don't dominate the conversation.

It is possible in a talk-it-over night to approach important subjects before they become problem areas. It is much better to say, "What would you do if your best friend offered you drugs?" or "If some really popular kids wanted you to cut school and hang out at the mall all afternoon, what would you do?" than to wish later you had discussed it.

Some other possible general topics are how to find God's will for your life, how to deal with temptation, what to do when someone swears at you or takes God's name in vain, how to react when someone calls you a "Sunday school boy," or how to have personal devotions.

Music Night. Plan a singing time with old and new songs. Musical innovations might include an "anything band" consisting of pots, pans, waxed paper on a comb, kazoos, harmonicas, and boxes to pound on like drums; tape recordings of your family singing together; puppets singing; favorite records; or Christian groups on video (available for renting from a Christian bookstore).

It doesn't matter whether the result is more noise than music. The important thing is the involvement of the whole family. The music can be secular or religious, old or new, action choruses or classical music or it can be a recital by a family member who is learning to play an instrument.

Reading Night. I'll talk more about reading later. It's an important family activity. Here I will just say that it is a good idea to spend an occasional family night reading together.

Show-and-Tell Night. Each family member shares something— a hobby, collection, object, an interesting incident, something he has seen or read, or even a favorite riddle or joke. Let each person share several things.

Surprise Night. Plan something that will be a complete surprise to the family, such as inviting a special guest to visit, showing photographs that the family has not yet seen, going on a treasure hunt, eating something delicious together, playing a new game, or going out to some new place.

At our house surprise night was always the favorite family night. Kids love to be surprised and to plan surprises for others. Sometimes our surprise was something as simple as going to a local shopping mall and then visiting an ice cream parlor. It doesn't have to be fancy; it just has to be unexpected.

> *A successful family council allows for open sharing.*

Family Council. Last, but certainly not least, is family council—a time for airing ideas and concerns. Plan topics that the entire family can discuss. These can be problem areas that need to be dealt with or constructive suggestions about how to improve family life. Topics could include behavior in church, things I wish you wouldn't do, finances, family chores, and vacation plans.

The secret to a successful family council is an atmosphere that allows for open sharing. Children should feel free to confront their parents about embarrassing things parents said to their friends, about talking to them like they were babies, about not letting them finish what they had to say before making a judgment call, and so on.

Parents must learn to take criticism from children and admit guilt when necessary. Likewise, the children have to learn to take criticism and admit their guilt when there are discussions of attitude problems, sloppiness in their rooms, not finishing chores, or laxness about homework. It is easier for children to admit their error when Mom and Dad are willing to do so.

Often during our family councils we discussed positive subjects with the children. We told them about financial goals we were trying to accomplish and how we stood on those projects. We laid plans for vacations and minitrips, and invited their input. We shared goals and dreams. In short, this was a family business meeting in which everyone had an equal voice and an equal vote. Although we had regularly scheduled times for family council, anyone in the family could call a spur-of-the-moment session whenever one was needed to discuss a pressing problem.

Family councils can help make family life go smoothly as members grow closer while airing their differences and sharing their dreams. People who share—care. Sharing helps families understand how each other is feeling.

Reading

Reading is a treasure that can be a part of every home. Parents who model reading and enjoying books will encourage their children to read. Reading together as a family will help children develop their skill while providing an experience of sharing that bonds the family together.

A child who is familiar with books has a head start on life. From books it is possible to learn about places you may never go and become familiar with people you will never meet. You can step backward through time and understand the peoples of past centuries. You can learn to make houses and gardens. You can learn to repair a car, design a garment, or teach a dog to obey. You can learn about the mysteries of space and the complex world of the cell. There is a book for every idea that enters your head. And it is through a particular book, the Bible, that you and your child will learn the path to eternal life.

Reading aloud provides a family with a forum for all kinds of discussion—first about the story, and then about the values of the people in the story, and later about your family's values on the same subject.

We cannot underestimate the importance of our personal influence on our children and their value system. If we are able to communicate with them, then we are able to communicate our values to them. And an excellent way to begin communicating is through reading aloud together and talking about what is read.

You can deliberately select a book that addresses a value you want to emphasize to your family. You may want to read a book about lying and then discuss it. A story about a disabled child would open the door to discussing the needs of the disabled and what our responsibility is toward them.

Finding Time for Family Reading

How do you find the time to read together as a family? You don't! You *make time* for reading. First you must ask yourself, Do I think it is important for our family to spend time reading together aloud? If the answer is yes, then you set aside time for it. Reading together as a family will never happen unless someone in your family is convinced that it is important.

Here are some ideas for finding time for family reading:

- Keep a book handy for those times when you must wait for others. Kids hate waiting and can become unbearable. A good story helps to speed the time for all of you.
- Read in the car when the family is traveling.
- Read to your children for ten or fifteen minutes just before their bedtime. Reading has a tremendously soothing effect. Watch out for the little rascals who beg for "just one more story."
- Set aside a special time each week for reading together as a family. Sunday afternoons or Saturday evenings are often times when little else is scheduled.
- Vacation times can be a time for reading something very special. Perhaps you'll find as we did that reading one book together generated the desire to read another. We saved

some of those books for vacations when we could spend an extended time reading.

- Remember that having a book with you, ready to be read, is better than many shelves of unread books at home.

What to Read

It isn't always easy to find books that appeal to all the age levels represented in a family. Some stories are enthralling to children, but become a real drag to the adults trying to wade through them. But when our family walked beside a young Labrador retriever, an old English bull terrier, and a Siamese cat as they ventured across the Canadian wilderness in a book called *The Incredible Journey,* no one's attention dwindled for a moment. And when at last Bodger, the old terrier, threw himself into the waiting arms of his young master, there wasn't a dry eye in the family.

Every family needs a good Bible storybook.

If you find a book you are reading is either too difficult for the younger members of the family or too inane for the adults, put it aside and choose something more to the tastes of everyone. We discovered that the stories did not necessarily have to be tailored to the youngest member of the family. Although the youngest in our family may not have understood every word of what was being said, he was able to catch the gist of it, and amazingly enough, some of those big words soon crept into his vocabulary.

Every family needs a good Bible storybook. Dozens of them are on the market. There is something quieting and comforting about reading Bible stories with your children. There is comfort to the child who learns that God is always there, watching over her, protecting her, and loving her. There is assurance to the parent who learns that God is pro-family, able to deliver, over all, and in control of all things. Families who read Bible stories together will grow in their inner beings.

I think there is also great value in reading fantasy to children. Children seem to have the ability to take fantasy in their own stride. Certainly they get gigantic doses of fantasy on television. In fact isn't almost everything they see on television fantasy? Yet even from fantastic, imaginary adventures, children are learning concepts of right and wrong and of good and evil. They learn facts, cultures, language styles, and how to follow the thread of a complex narrative. Fantasy can be tremendously mind expanding, causing the readers and the listeners to think more broadly and more creatively than they have in the past.

Some of the great classics of children's literature fall into the realm of fantasy. C. S. Lewis's *Chronicles of Narnia* series, J. R. R. Tolkien's *The Lord of the Rings,* and George MacDonald's writings are fantasy. So are *Alice in Wonderland, Gulliver's Travels,* and many others.

Family reading should encompass a broad spectrum of literature. It should include history (told at a child's level), adventure stories, poetry, biographies, humorous pieces, and animal stories. There should be picture books, including pop-up books. There should be rhyming books, books that play with words, easy-reader books, and books written in words that paint glowing landscapes for the mind.

Using TV to Instill Values

With all the negative talk about television, this section's title might startle you. Can TV really be used to instill values? Yes, I think it can, *but* it takes some serious consideration.

The major problem with television from a shared experience standpoint is that it isn't shared. TV has become our entertainment, our baby-sitter, our company. In some homes the TV is always on, regardless of what's on and whether anyone is actually watching it. It just keeps up its incessant din in the background.

If television is to become a shared family experience, then everyone in the family must sit down together and view the programs. Right there we create an interesting problem. First, the family must agree about what program to watch. Communication, compromise, and cooperation come into play almost instantly when the family begins to discuss what to watch.

The other problem with television is that it is an observer activity, not a participatory one. Did you ever notice that people on

TV usually are not sitting around watching TV? How boring that would be. We like to watch TV because the characters are interacting. The more action, the better we like it.

For TV to be a shared experience with some interaction between family members, you must find a way to make it participatory. One way is to talk about what you are seeing. Rather than watching the screen until your eyeballs are fried, how about watching one program and then turning it off and talking about what you have viewed?

There are some fine, family-oriented programs on TV today—programs that portray your values. But sometimes programs that have been okay all year will run something that will make your hair stand on end. Sometimes it involves the occult, the New Age, or a different set of moral values than your family espouses.

Because you have grown to trust the program, you aren't expecting this problem. Suddenly, there it is. It is important to say to your kids right then, "You know, the Bible has something to say about this" or "Those are the values of the person who wrote the script, but our family believes . . ." or "In our family we don't do that." Then you'll have to decide whether it is bad enough to turn off the TV at that moment, or whether it is all right to watch until the end of the program and then talk about it.

Watch for subtle put-downs of fathers, parents, and women. Watch for the sexually suggestive and talk about it right then. Watch for derogatory words like *nerd, dumbo,* and *idiot*. Point out the differences between what's being portrayed and your own stand on important issues.

At the same time applaud television that stands up for moral values. There are some excellent series that consistently tackle problem areas for young people such as drugs, smoking, stealing, and premarital sex.

Wisdom says that we must control TV; we can't let it control us. Invest weekly in a *TV Guide* and look through it as soon as you get it. Before viewing time, choose the programming appropriate for your family. In other words, don't just watch everything that comes on but select what you are going to see.

Over the years TV has become increasingly immoral, increasingly blatant, and more insulting to our intelligence. How much of that is enough for your family? Each family needs to decide about TV and its use in the home. But please, do decide to take some kind of action regarding TV. Use it wisely and well. Make it a shared experience, especially with younger children.

Ask yourself these questions to discover whether you are controlling TV or it's controlling you:

- Are household members watching TV rather than doing assigned tasks—such as homework or chores?
- Would the family rather stay home and watch television than go to church?
- Do family activities seem boring? Would members rather watch television than participate in a family activity?
- Have TV personalities and characters, even fictional ones, become a main topic of family conversation?
- Is there conflict over which program to watch?
- Does something that would have shocked you once no longer shock you?
- Has TV become a baby-sitter?
- Would people rather stay up and watch late-night TV than go to bed at a reasonable time?

It is important to know where the off switch is on our television sets and to use it, even amidst howls of protest. If you can't control TV, you might consider storing it in a closet and bringing it out only for special programs. We have found that when our television viewing is controlled and carefully selected, we enjoy the little we see ten times more than we would if we watched everything. Try it. After a few days of withdrawal, you may even like the change.

As children grow older, there comes a time for the parents to let go in lots of areas, and TV is one. Now is the time to see if what you taught them will stick. Give them time. Remember it may take a while for them to find their own way. The chances they will make right choices are increased if you have watched television with them and if they have a strong set of values.

Dinnertime

Dinner can be one of the best times for the family to share and communicate on a daily basis. However, I suspect that the American family's dinnertime is almost nonexistent in many homes. I imagine that the kids grab something on their way to a sports activity and Dad reaches home long after other family members have eaten and gone out again.

I heard about a family who sold their dining room table because no one used it anymore. All of their eating was done from trays in front of the TV. The mother in the family cooked a big pot of something and left it on the stove. Whenever anyone was hungry, he or she dished up something and sat down in front of the TV to eat it.

Good food, pretty dishes, flowers, or family discussions can make dinner special.

What a tragedy to lose this special time when family members can touch base and share what has happened throughout the day! What a shame to lose one of the times when kind gestures can be done for other members of the family—gestures such as special foods, pretty dishes, flowers, and maybe even candlelight!

It takes such little effort to make dinner special: cloth or even lovely paper napkins, beautiful but inexpensive glassware, practical but lovely flatware and dishes, or a candle. An inexpensive candle can add such a festive air. A few flowers from the grocery store can make a meal seem special. Even a simple bowl of fruit looks pretty and helps lend an elegant air to the table.

Food can be special, too, because even if Mom works, there are wonderful dishes that can be prepared in minutes. Almost any food anyone could want now comes ready to eat in a few minutes. Even if you don't use prepared foods, many homes have microwaves that cook food quickly. There really is no excuse for sloppy, uninteresting, unappealing food preparation. Here is a time when the cook can say, "I care" with such little effort.

And Mom doesn't have to do all the cooking either. Even small children can and should be taught to help. They can learn how to set a pretty table. Everyone needs to pitch in and help, especially if everyone in the family works or goes to school.

When a family is seated around a table at dinner, it's the ideal time to teach proper table manners. (Your children will thank you for that knowledge when they are grown.) And it's a great time for family discussions. I heard about two families, each of which did something unique. In one, the father asked the children each evening what new thing they had learned that day. He expected them to have an answer for him. Just before dinner youngsters could be seen thumbing through an encyclopedia to look for something to report. In another family, the father asked what new word the children had learned that day. Here the children used the dictionary every day to find a new word to share. Those families built knowledgeable, alert, observant people.

You may want to include these ideas in your family's schedule, or you may want to come up with some ideas that are unique to your family. People—including children—like to share what is happening in their world. Parents need to encourage individual feelings and independent thinking. At our table our children should be safe to express feelings and independent thoughts.

During dinner you may hear things you will not hear at any other time. You may hear your children's friends' values being mouthed back by your children. Right then with a few simple words—maybe with some questions to help your child evaluate what he has just told you—you can realign *your* values in your child.

Mealtime should be a pleasant, happy time of sharing over God's good gifts of food, family, shelter, and peace. Try to keep it so in your home. Sometimes, because everyone is filled with the stresses of the day, mealtime is anything but peaceful and happy. Strive for peace if at all possible.

Treasured Guests

I think entertaining others in your home is one of the finest activities for a family.

In the first place, it is a biblical concept: "thereby some have entertained angels unawares" (Heb. 13:2 KJV). The idea of hospitality is found throughout the Bible. In the oriental culture of the Bible, the attitude toward hospitality was that once a guest entered your home, everything you had was his. It was as if he owned it, which is a bit further than most of us want to go.

Bringing others into your home can be a wonderful learning experience for your children. Your table can literally become the crossroads of the world. Colleges and universities are full of international students who would love to be invited to an American home, and there are some American kids who are away from home for the first time and would enjoy a home-cooked meal.

There are people who travel for a living who would be delighted to spend a night in a home instead of in yet another hotel. There are business associates who would respond in a relaxed, positive way if they could share a meal at our table. There are artists and musicians and storytellers who could bring delight and wonder to our children's lives. There are older people who feel life has gone on without them and they no longer have value to anyone. Think about inviting some senior adults to your home to share with your family. Their stories of life in earlier times will stretch your children's imagination and broaden their understanding of the past.

Invite families with children the same age as your children. We used to have so much company that if we ever ate alone on a Sunday, the kids complained that we never had company. They were complaining because they enjoyed guests. It's good for families to have fellowship with other families.

Invite your pastor and his family to your home. Get to know them as people. They are just like you. They laugh, they cry, they get hurt, they enjoy success, and they suffer failure. And believe it or not, they may not get asked to their parishioners' homes as often as you think they do.

Your children will have a new perspective on the man who stands in the pulpit each Sunday if they can see him up close and in their own home. They will admire him if you are consistent in what is said about him on the days when he is not in your home. Teach your children to value your church and its leaders.

Invite other interesting people to your home. Do you know a nurse, a guitar teacher, an actress, a drummer, a painter, or a foreign-born person living in your community? Bring these people into your home one at a time and let your children talk with them. If you know that the person has something he can do or show, ask him to bring it along so the kids can experience his talent.

A young man we befriended was an expert at both juggling and using a yo-yo. He often entertained us at home. Some people are great storytellers. Some are rock or coin collectors. All have something with which to enrich your children's lives and light a spark in them.

Value people, value their talent, and value relationships with these people. Let your children share in their lives, and let them share in your children's lives. If you make your home and your table a place of hospitality, your children will learn the value of hospitality and will become hospitable people. But more than that, each guest adds to your child's life something that no one can take away.

Invite interesting people to your home.

Entertaining others is a little bit of work, but the rewards far outweigh the labor. Entertaining—which usually involves food in some way—can be as expensive or inexpensive as you make it. During the lean times of my life, our work necessitated a lot of entertaining. I love company, so I never got tired of cooking for these guests.

Early on I decided that anyone who dropped by the house just before or during dinner was welcome to join us at the table, but he had to eat whatever I was fixing. I never had anyone turn down the food being served.

Usually when I invited guests, I tried to make it a special time. Menus were often a little more elaborate, but not always. I distinctly remember a time when a minister friend, who was conducting a seminar at our church, was with us for dinner. I don't remember why, but I served him stew. It was a good stew with lots of fresh vegetables, and I probably served some kind of homemade bread with it. I remember how that man ate and how he enjoyed it. He commented that now that his children were grown, his wife hardly ever fixed stew, and he missed it.

Stew is not an expensive dish, but seasoned well, served with flair and with an air of hospitality that says, "You're welcome here, and I want to share what we have with you," it is a memorable meal. It has been my experience that when the atmosphere of a home shouts, "You're welcome here," people almost forget what they are eating. I guess if it were terrible food, they would notice, but what you serve may not be as important as how you serve it.

If you can't afford a full meal, why not serve dessert and coffee? What about lunch or breakfast? What about a popcorn and video night for teenagers? Or a cookie bake-off for younger kids who are then allowed to eat all the cookies they want?

Another way to entertain with style is to serve ethnic food. Many ethnic cultures feature inexpensive food. Spaghetti or lasagna, served with a big tossed salad and bread sticks on a red-and-white-checked cloth by candlelight, can be as much fun as a crown roast of pork dinner.

Just a word about table settings. Good food in good company served on paper plates will be enjoyed, but it is also possible to acquire flatware, dishes, glassware, tablecloths, napkins, and all the other niceties rather inexpensively. Most of these things can be acquired through garage sales, import stores, estate sales, and department store closeouts.

When it is necessary to count the cost of entertaining guests, remember to keep it simple and do it with style. It may be nice to have a formal bouquet on the table, but it is less expensive to use cut flowers, decorative grasses, colored leaves, or pine boughs from your garden, which have been arranged informally. Such simple table arrangements were made popular by Jacqueline Kennedy when she was First Lady. If it's good enough for the White House, it's good enough for my house.

A friend told me that she uses lots of candles when entertaining. She said low lights and candlelight add a wonderful charm and can hide all kinds of things, such as shabby carpet or less-than-perfect furniture.

A fire in the fireplace is an inviting focal point. Lately I've been inviting friends to come for lunch. I like to spread it out in front of the fire in the living room. I cover a little tea table with a white cloth, add a candle and maybe a tiny bouquet of flowers, and we sit, talking the afternoon away. It's very pleasant.

Successful entertaining is as simple as creating and communicating an attitude that says, I'm glad you've come to see me. I want this to be a special time for us to remember, because you're very important to me. Though what I have may be simple and I may not have very much, I'll share what I have with you because you are my friend.

3
Collecting Waterfalls without a Jar

"Awww! If you've seen one waterfall, you've seen them all," a friend told us one day. "Don't you get tired of looking at waterfalls?"

"Nope," we told him.

"How many waterfalls are you hoping to collect?" he asked.

"Just as many as we can reach in a lifetime."

People collect salt and pepper shakers, rocks, baseball caps, fishing lures, all kinds of treasures. People like to collect things. We decided that our family would collect waterfalls. You don't need a jar to collect a waterfall but you do have to work to make this collection. About the only way to collect a waterfall is to get out and hike, so that's what we decided to do. We hiked and took photos, and that's how we built our collection. (If you live in a city and never get near a waterfall, stay with me. I have some ideas for city dwellers too.)

At first, we took little half-mile to one-mile treks back into the woods. On the way we looked at foliage, flowers, rocks, trees, seedpods, and mushrooms. The woods became as familiar to us as our own backyard. If there were berries, we walked slowly, eating our way along the trail. Usually we tried to wait to eat our official lunch until we reached the falls but sometimes we stopped along the way to eat. I think we sometimes ate more than we walked.

When we arrived at the falls we took pictures. Each waterfall has its own unique setting. We could get behind some of them and look out through the water. Some waterfalls shot tons of spray into the air and gave us a fair soaking. Some had deep pools at their base, and some had shallow bubbling streams. Some of the waterfalls came down in a sheet of water, and some divided into two streams midway. Some were blue-white with glacial silt, and some fell thousands of feet to a shelf and then continued cascading down the mountain.

A really tough hike was to Comet Falls, Washington State's highest waterfall. To reach it you have to hike to an elevation of 1,900 feet in two and a half miles. You climb up and up switchbacks for about a mile, then—still climbing—you traverse a boulder-strewn meadow. At times the path squeezes between the boulders. After wading a stream, you climb one more hill, make one more turn—and there it is—350 feet of thunder pounding onto the rocks below. This is one of those spray-casting, rainbow-producing waterfalls. We were so hot by the time we arrived that we stood in the spray and let it soak us.

I'll never forget the experience we shared with the kids' grandfather in Montana at a little stream that originates in a hot springs. After flowing across meadows for miles the water still is warm when it cascades over a cliff. Someone has dammed up the stream below the falls and made a wading pool. Grandpa and the kids stood in the warm water beneath the falls and took the pounding of their lives—all the while laughing and laughing.

Why so much fuss about waterfalls? It isn't the waterfalls. It isn't the hiking. It's the shared experience of being together and gathering, not waterfalls, but memories. People who hike together learn how to talk to each other. People who sit together, eating a sandwich and viewing God's magnificent handiwork, have to work very hard at carrying a grudge. The shared experience draws a family closer.

What Can Your Family Collect?

What can your family collect without a jar? The possibilities are unending. There are thousands of places and ways to collect experiences, and so much of it doesn't need to cost you one cent. But it will cost you some effort and time. In exchange, you receive wonderful memories and experiences for your family.

Rocks. Kids like to collect rocks—pretty-colored ones, heart-shaped rocks, round, smooth rocks, and plain, gray, ugly rocks—for reasons only they know.

Rockhounding, however, is a hobby that many adults enjoy. If this appeals to you and your family, find out where the local rock hounds do their collecting and what it is they are gathering. Maybe you'll want to invest in a small rock tumbler. Even plain beach pebbles become beautiful when highly polished.

One kind of rock to collect is agates. They can be found in streambeds, on ocean beaches, in fields, and in gravel banks. There are blue agates, moss agates, beautiful banded agates from the shores of Lake Superior in Minnesota, and probably lots of other kinds of agates available all over this country.

Seashells. You can look for seashells on every ocean beach in the country.

Geodes. You can collect geodes in Montana, Arizona, Oregon, and many other places. We used to pick up geodes when I was a kid. It was fun to look for the small, round, pockmarked stones. Then Dad would break them open with a hammer so that we could see the crystal-filled interior.

Birds. You can collect birds with a camera or in your memory. When we were at the Grand Canyon, we watched eight or ten western bluebirds drinking and splashing about in the drinking fountain. Bluebirds are rather a rare sight these days, unless you know where to look. We can take you to a meadow where almost every fence post bears a bluebird house and hundreds of birds are engaged in their busy activities.

On a short hike we watched a rather large bird swooping and diving over a small lake. We thought that it might be the rather rare osprey, a fish hawk, but we weren't sure. In fascination, we watched his airborne choreography. In a few minutes a ranger came along and confirmed that it was indeed an osprey. What a wonderful experience to share as a family!

We all treasure a time when we drove up a river where the bald eagles spend the winter. Dozens of them were in the trees and riding the wind currents. Some of them were on a sandbar devouring the fish they had caught in the river. It would be a thrill for almost anyone to see one bald eagle, the symbol of our national heritage, but to see dozens was memorable indeed.

If you can't get to the country, don't worry. Cities are full of birds. Don't despise starlings, sparrows, pigeons, crows, blackbirds, magpies, and other city-dwelling birds. Take the time as a family to learn how many of these birds came to live in this country. It is very interesting.

One of the positive aspects about collecting birds, flowers, or whatever is that you never know when you'll be able to add to your collection. It can happen unexpectedly. Once when we were driving through the fog on our way to San Francisco, Canada geese suddenly fell from the sky and landed on every available inch of water. A huge migratory flight had been caught in the fog, and the geese were being forced down to rest and feed. It was a rare and wonderful sight, and one I always hoped I'd see repeated but never have.

Visit a local nursery seasonally.

Flowers. Walk through a vacant city lot—and look small. Some of the tiny plants at your feet bear minuscule flowers with wonderful markings and coloring. We have seen some that resemble orchids. Flowers this small often are overlooked because of their size. But small children like small things, and if the whole family can sit down in a weedy, vacant lot and examine a patch of earth, you will see things you never have seen before. It may well be your child who discovers them for you.

Walk in the woods at different times of the year and watch for flowers you have never seen. Buy a book that identifies wildflowers. Gather blossoms, but only if the flowers are plentiful and if it's all right to do so where you are walking. Press them between paper towels in the pages of a book until they are dry. Then your family will have a visible reminder of a shared experience.

You can collect flower memories by visiting a park, a test garden, or a farm where flowers are grown for seed. Visit a bulb farm. Visit orchid houses, begonia gardens, or poinsettia farms. Visit a conservatory in a park. Conservatories often house banana plants, orchids, cactuses, seasonal flowers, flowering vines, and all kinds of unusual plants. What a treat to step out of a wintry day into the tropical environment of a conservatory! For a few minutes you can pretend you are basking in the sun on a tropical island.

Visit a local nursery seasonally. In early spring one of the big nurseries in our area is filled with primroses of every color. Later there are seemingly acres of geraniums, petunias, and roses. Then come the chrysanthemums of every hue imaginable, and finally poinsettias blazing away—row upon row—red, white, and pink.

Museums. You can collect museums. Almost every town and village in the country has some kind of museum, and each one has a distinctive flavor.

Native American museums are abundant throughout the country. There are industrial, air, historical, and mining museums. Some museums feature futuristic artwork and displays. Open-air museums demonstrate the lifestyles of different historical periods. There are museums attached to candy factories, near schools, and in ghost towns. In some instances, whole towns are a kind of museum: Virginia City, Montana; Cripple Creek, Colorado; Greenfield Village, Michigan; and Williamsburg, Virginia, are worth visiting.

And of course, there's the granddaddy museum of them all, the Smithsonian, which really is a collection of museums. It would not be hard to spend weeks viewing everything on display. A favorite for children at the Smithsonian is the Natural History Building, which has a live insect collection. Children are allowed to hold the bugs on their fingers. Some of the bugs look like something out of a space movie, and some of them hiss and make other strange noises. Others glow with iridescent colors.

If you live in southern California, the museum at Long Beach that houses Howard Hughes's Spruce Goose is worth a visit as is a stop at the museum's neighbor, the *Queen Mary.*

Art Galleries. You can collect art galleries. Many small cities have art galleries. Visit them and see what they offer—impressionistic paintings, old masters, early American primitives, or some other style. All large cities have at least one, and usually several, art galleries.

Wait until children are school-age to take them to art galleries. By then they will be thrilled to see the original works of art that are pictured in their school textbooks or that they have seen on television.

Some galleries will let you take pictures as long as you don't use a flash. Others strictly forbid photographs. Ask an employee about the gallery's photo policy. You may be able to gather works of art with your camera to later view and discuss as a family.

Most art museums also have shops where you can buy inexpensive postcards and reproductions of the kids' favorite paintings. Buy them. Frame them and hang them in your home as an opportunity for remembering your shared experience of visiting the gallery and for influencing your children's value of art.

The National Gallery of Art at the Smithsonian houses one of the finest collections of impressionistic paintings in the world. It is also filled with American art treasures and hundreds and hundreds of superb masterpieces from around the world. Here you can purchase fine reproductions on an excellent paper that are inexpensive.

Architecture. Even if you live in a small town, you can experience much together as a family simply by becoming aware of your surroundings. The little town where I was born had some beautiful homes, but I hardly noticed them back then. It wasn't until I grew up, moved away, and then returned to visit that I really saw them. There was a European-style chateau and a Spanish-style house. The front of one home had an elk head mounted and displayed under glass. A two-story brick mansion just down the street had belonged to a Civil War general. We called it the Haunted House.

Several years ago we purchased a book that describes architecture in our area. It also relates the history of many of the buildings. It is great fun to walk through a neighborhood and read about the various houses or buildings on a block. Reading that book has taught us to look up beyond the remodeled storefronts. When you look up, you see all kinds of interesting things—including gargoyles, lions, and other creatures.

There is a wonderful building in Seattle that is called the Arctic Building. All around the facade, about fifteen feet high, are walrus heads. Many years ago after a severe earthquake the tusks were removed to keep them from falling to the street below. They have since been restored to the building.

Charitable groups often persuade owners of lovely old and unique homes to open them to the public once a year. They charge a small admission fee. Other old homes belong to the state and are open for viewing throughout the year. Most of these are furnished in period furnishings. It's fun to see the interesting tools and furnishings our recent ancestors used in their daily life. Take pictures, keep a notebook, and see how many old houses and antique items of interest you can collect.

Neighborhood Walks

Regardless of where we are traveling, we enjoy stopping at some village or small town, getting out of the car, and walking. It's most fun if a street fair or a farmers' market is in progress. If not, we begin searching for the local bakery or specialty shops.

Once we spent a night in Rome, New York, and were enchanted by this city's Italian flavor. We were delighted to find gelato (Italian ice cream) shops, fresh pasta hanging in shop windows, and a *bols* (a European game played with weighted balls) tournament in progress right behind our motel. Here was a bit of the old country's traditions being remembered in America.

Most cities are made up of many neighborhoods, each with its own flavor and identity. Those neighborhoods are places to go exploring. Visit the shops, walk the streets, talk to longtime residents, and listen to the sounds of that neighborhood—streetcars, buses, trolleys, church bells, and factory whistles. Use all your senses to learn about this new area. Eat borscht in a Russian restaurant or croissants and crepes at a French restaurant or have high tea in an English tearoom. All of these places can be found in most cities.

Getting Ready to Go

One-day outings should be relaxed, fun times of sharing experiences. A little preparation and thought can ensure they are. Here's a short checklist for day-trippers and hikers.

Shoes. Forget fashion and wear comfortable walking shoes. Blisters are no fun, so if there is the slightest possibility anyone will develop a blister, bring along Band-Aids or better still, adhesive moleskin. The minute anyone feels a hot spot, stop immediately and apply moleskin to it.

Backpack. Even for city walkers, a backpack is a useful place to tuck all kinds of things.

Jackets or sweaters. "Always be prepared" is a good motto. Every year people die of hypothermia because they are unprepared for a sudden shift in the weather. It doesn't have to be very cold for people, especially children, to suffer hypothermia, which occurs when the body loses heat faster than it can replace it. Hypothermia can result in extreme shaking, disorientation, and death. Getting soaked hastens the process.

A wool sweater and a raincoat, or even a large plastic bag that can be worn as a raincoat, tucked into the backpack is good insurance against hypothermia. Even when wet, wool helps the body retain heat.

Food. Little people (and big people too) don't have much fun if they are hungry. Carry snacks and dispense them lavishly. Fruit is heavy to carry but makes a good snack. Granola bars and dried fruit are also good snacks.

Take drinking water along if you won't be able to purchase drinks. Never drink from streams and rivers. Even in the remotest places, they are polluted because there are so many hikers. Drinking polluted water can make you extremely ill.

Camera. If you're going to collect without a jar, you'll need a camera and a notebook.

Physical preparation. Start easy, start slow, and start walking around your neighborhood before you attempt a walk in the woods. Hiking can make muscles that are unaccustomed to exercise scream out in protest. Getting out of bed the day after a major hike can be a painful experience.

Don't overdo it when small children are along for the adventure. They will feel just as much accomplishment from a short walk in the woods as from a major hike. Stop often to talk and look around. After all, that's why you came. These are not overachiever events; they are family sharing times.

Mental preparation. Planning can be half the fun. Prepare family members by telling them several days ahead of the event where the family is going. Talk about it the day of the event and on the way.

Collecting waterfalls, pickle factories, bugs, and elephants without a jar are opportunities to celebrate being together as a family. You will get to know each other's strengths and weaknesses and you will have many meaningful experiences that you will talk about in the future.

What will your family collect?

4

A Fiddler on Your Roof

Creating Family Traditions

Traditions are an important part of family life. We can learn much from Tevya of *Fiddler on the Roof* about when to bend tradition and when bending would destroy something valuable. Tradition builds strength into our families, a sense of the continuity of our family, and stability in a rapidly changing world.

Maybe the reason children and even adults like tradition so much is that it gives them something to anticipate. "Always" events, something we *always* do a certain time of year, or even "always" nights (I have a friend who *always* served spaghetti on Thursday nights) build tradition into our families.

Children, particularly young ones, love repetition. They love to hear the same story over and over again. And they love events that they can look forward to year after year. In this chapter we will discuss celebrating everything, and in the next chapter we will talk about celebrating the big holidays—Christmas, Easter, and Thanksgiving.

Establishing Your Own Traditions

It is important to bring into your own family some of the traditions of each set of grandparents. Even though you will want to keep some of those old family traditions, it also is important to establish new traditions.

We've watched young couples try so hard to please their parents and extended families—by running here and there on holidays, birthdays, and anniversaries—that they never have taken the time to establish traditions just for their own children in their own home. At some point couples need to say, "No, Mom and Dad, we're not coming this year. We're going to have Christmas at home this time. It's time for us to establish our own traditions. We'll see you later on during the holidays."

As children grow older, it is important to modify or bend some of your traditions to fit the changing needs of your children and of the whole family. Flexibility is probably the most important characteristic in a parent. Parents must know when to let go of and when to keep a tradition. If your teenager has outgrown something you have always done, let it go, and don't make a federal case out of letting it go. Maybe it's time to stop giving her an Easter basket or insisting she spend every Sunday afternoon at Aunt Millie's just because you've always spent Sunday afternoons at Aunt Millie's.

I remember the year when I returned home from a long business trip just two days before Thanksgiving. The thought of preparing a Thanksgiving dinner overwhelmed me, so we decided to go out for dinner. That's not very traditional in our family. But guess what? We all look back to that Thanksgiving as one of the best we ever had.

We chose a dining room high atop a hotel overlooking the city. The food was superb and the variety endless. We all ate what we wanted. And the real bonus was that there were no dishes to wash. We just sat and talked with each other. We enjoyed it so much that

> Modify traditions to meet the changing needs of your family.

we have done it a couple of times since then. Who says Thanksgiving dinner has to be eaten at home with two dozen relatives?

Celebrating Everything

One way tradition can be built is by celebrating everything—and I mean everything. Celebrate with an elaborate party or celebrate quietly but celebrate life.

The following is a list of celebration ideas. But please don't stop here. Think of the other days and ways you can celebrate life with your children. Make living at your house fun.

January

New Year's Day once was a time for holding open house and inviting friends to stop by, but those days probably are gone forever. For most families New Year's Day means football and football and football.

Even if viewing football is to be the order of the day, it is always more fun when family or friends are invited in to cheer along, even if they are cheering a rival team. Football on TV can be a shared experience if Dad or Mom, whichever is the fan, takes the time to explain to the kids what is happening and to convey his or her love of the game.

Martin Luther King Day is an important holiday. It is a good time to discuss the contribution African Americans have made to our society. Because Martin Luther King Jr. is a modern-day hero, it is possible to find a great deal of information about him. Television stations often replay footage of his life, his famous speeches, and his tragic death. You'll find many books about Dr. King in your local library.

Use this day to emphasize the value all people have in God's sight, regardless of their race or color. God loves all people, and your kids need to know that. Of course, if this is not your attitude throughout the year, one day of talking about it won't have much effect.

Another idea for this day is to use the model of Dr. King's "I Have a Dream" speech, and talk about your family's dreams and vision for the future.

Snow Day. If you live in an area where it snows, why not celebrate it? Plan a winter picnic of chili in an oversized thermos, sandwiches, hot chocolate, and cookies. Dress warmly, find a sheltered place in the sunshine, and enjoy being together as a family.

Play in the snow with the kids, go sledding, build a snowman, lie in the snow and make snow angels.

February

Groundhog Day. Research the legends associated with this day. Make sure your children understand that they are only legends and are just for fun. Before the day arrives, assign them the task of watching for interesting items about groundhogs in newspapers and on television. They can share these. A prize could be given to the child who finds the most information about groundhogs or Groundhog Day.

Valentine's Day is an ideal time to have a special dinner. Flowers and candles make it especially nice. Finish the meal with heart-shaped cookies, a heart-shaped cake, or even a heart-shaped box of candy from the store.

Young children will enjoy making valentines to give to each family member.

Older children may want to discover the real meaning of Valentine's Day. Actually, very little is known about Saint Valentine himself. He was martyred on February 14, 270 A.D. The day has been celebrated since the seventh century, and because the day is around the same time birds begin mating, someone decided it would be a good day for young people to choose lovers. Thus the customs relating to hearts, cupids, and love were born.

President's Day affords your family a time for talking about the value of our governmental system. It can be a patriotic day of flag waving for your family. Sing patriotic songs. Read a story about George Washington or Abraham Lincoln. Cook a recipe from colonial or Civil War times.

Susan B. Anthony Day. Find out the contribution Susan Anthony made and share this information with the family. If possible have a Susan B. Anthony dollar to show the children.

March

Lion and Lamb Festival. Since March is supposed to either come in like a lion and leave like a lamb or vice versa, celebrate the event.

Discuss the ways in which Jesus Christ is like a lion or a lamb. Use a concordance to look up references. You may want to read a passage from *The Chronicles of Narnia* in which C. S. Lewis depicts Christ as the lion Aslan.

You may want to include in your festival some family kite flying. Real fun can be had with a two-handled model, which can be made to dip and whirl. You can buy a kite for each person and hook them together in a chain. If you haven't visited a kite store for a while, you are in for a treat. Take the kids with you when you shop. You'll find beautiful kites of all shapes and sizes. A good kite will last for years if properly cared for, so invest the money if you possibly can.

St. Patrick's Day. Every year a kind of madness settles in around the middle of March. The madness has a name—St. Patrick's Day. In our area the celebrating grows a little more lively every year, but you wouldn't want your family to participate in most of that celebrating.

Still, you can have fun together as a family. At our house St. Patrick's Day called for a special meal celebration. We had corned beef and cabbage, something green to drink (usually lime drink), and something called grasshopper pie, which is much better than it sounds.

Celebrate the coming of spring.

The legends surrounding St. Patrick, for whom this day was named, are many. St. Patrick really did exist and he really did live in Ireland, although he was English. He was captured as a boy by the Irish. After six years he escaped. A series of miracles are said to have occurred when Patrick prayed. Eventually he returned to Ireland, where he was made a bishop.

First Day of Spring. If ever there was a day to celebrate, it is the coming of spring. Plant some flowers together, go for a walk, find a pond and see if there are any baby ducks or tadpoles yet, go to a park and run, play ball together, visit a farm and see the new lambs, colts, or calves.

A research dairy near us allows visitors in its maternity barn. I still get a thrill when I see a newborn calf wobble its first few steps toward its mother. We always hoped we'd be there when a calf actually was being born. Once we arrived just minutes afterward, but we never were there at the actual moment of birth.

April

April Fools' Day. Who can start off April without at least one prank? Children love to celebrate this day. Help them think up fun, nondestructive pranks to pull on other family members. Let them dress up in polka dots and stripes—anything wild and crazy—and wear funny paper hats at dinner. Play silly, noisy games. Have fun!

Arbor Day is a day that goes almost unnoticed on our calendars. Traditionally it has been set aside for the planting of trees. So in honor of the occasion, plant a tree. Your children may know more about this holiday than you do, as it is often promoted through schools. If your kids have talked about it at school, let them teach you.

Time Change Day. This is the time change we all hate because we have to get up one hour earlier, and it always happens on Sunday. Why not plan a special breakfast and serve it in an unusual spot in the house—like on Mom and Dad's bed, or before a roaring fire, or outside if you live in a warm area? Or perhaps you could take everyone out to breakfast before church.

May

May Day can be a delightful celebration, a time of giving. Children can make little paper baskets with handles, fill them with garden flowers and maybe a cookie or a few candies, and early in the morning hang them on the neighbors' doors. Then they ring the doorbell and run.

Mother's Day is one of the big holidays of the year. Let the children decide what they will do to honor their mother. Dad needs to help make their wishes come true. If they are too young to be aware of the specialness of this day, he also needs to talk with them about Mother's Day and help the children find a way to show how much they value their mother.

This can be a tough holiday for single moms. Let the children surprise you, even though you may be aware of what they are planning and even if their plans may result in a messy house. Be truly grateful for their clumsy efforts. As time goes on, they will treasure you more and they will begin to realize what you have given of yourself to make their lives good. In time they will find a better way to reward you.

Single fathers need to encourage their children to honor their mother.

Memorial Day is a day for remembering. The apostle Paul encouraged Timothy to remember what he had been taught as a youth. Memorial Day can be a time for remembering those who've lived before us. This is a good day to look at old photos and learn more about your family's history. It also is a good time for taking children to visit graves of loved ones and talking about those who've gone to heaven ahead of us.

Memorial Day is a day for remembering.

Many towns have Memorial Day parades with a lot of military activity. Explain what this is all about to your children. Go on a picnic. Spend this day together getting to know one another better so that you are building your own memories.

June

Flag Day. This day will be more meaningful to your family if you fly a flag from your house or in your yard. Flag Day is set aside to commemorate the June 14, 1777, adoption by the Continental Congress of a resolution to make the Stars and Stripes the official flag of the United States.

Recite the pledge of allegiance together and sing the national anthem. Talk about why we stand at attention when this song is played. Once again, your school-aged children probably will know more about this holiday than you do. Learn from them.

Father's Day is Dad's special day, and now it is Mom's privilege to lead her children in honoring their father. Plan a special meal of his favorite foods, serve him breakfast in bed, or take him out to eat. Suggest that the children learn a poem or a Scripture verse about fathers and recite it to their dad.

In a home headed by a single mother, children should be encouraged to spend the day with their father, if that is appropriate. Single moms need to be supportive of the children's father. Nothing good will come from instilling bitterness in the children toward their father no matter what has happened in the past.

Have a devotional time and talk about the fatherhood of God. Help your children see God as a tender dad who loves them and expects obedience from them. Teach your children to respect both their earthly father and their heavenly Father.

First Day of Summer. Celebrate the longest day of the year. Go on a picnic, even an impromptu picnic if it is a weekday. Just pick up dinner and take it to a park. Picnics do not have to consist of traditional picnic food. It is possible to make a picnic from your regular dinner or pick up fast food on the way. After a few minutes outdoors, frayed nerves will disappear and cranky kids begin to have fun playing with each other.

Celebrate the longest day of the year with a picnic.

The first day of summer is a good time to let the kids stay up until sunset, regardless of how late it is.

July

Independence Day. The only holiday in July is Independence Day. This is a good time to fly your American flag. If you allow your children to have their own fireworks, then help them purchase them and supervise their use. Or go to the city's fireworks display.

Talk about what it means to be a free people, and give thanks to God that we are free. Discuss the cost of our freedom and how we can maintain it by being good citizens.

Spend the day with family and friends. Use the time to draw closer together as a family.

August

Friendship Day. August is the only month without a traditional holiday, so someone invented Friendship Day. If you have never celebrated this day, then here's your chance. Think of something to do to encourage friendship—having a block party in your neighborhood, sending homemade cards to friends, or letting the children invite a special friend to spend the day or night. Talk together about the value of a good friend.

September

Labor Day is the last holiday of the summer. Why not do something special, such as a short trip, a picnic, a bike ride, or something you have been wanting to do for a long time.

This would be an excellent time to discuss the new school year. You could talk together about your expectations of grades to be earned. You could pray together about the new teachers. You could discuss any fears kids may be having about the school year ahead. You may even suggest some events or awards for excellent grades.

Grandparents' Day is a fairly new holiday and a worthwhile one. Help your children think of ways to honor their grandparents. They could call their grandparents and express their love, make or buy a special card, or make a thank-you book. A time of special prayer for grandparents would be appropriate.

Beginning of Fall. Celebrate fall with a leaf-raking-and-burning party, if it is allowed in your area. Go for a walk and kick the leaves. Gather colored leaves and award a prize to the person finding the most beautiful leaf. Pick apples and let the kids help you make an apple pie. Sit on a hillside and listen to the quiet of an autumn day. Watch for flights of geese and other birds headed south for the winter.

October

Columbus Day. Read together about Columbus. Trace his route on a world map or globe. Discuss what it would be like to venture to a place where no one ever has been. Compare his journey to that of the first astronauts to the moon. Read in the Bible about Abraham starting off for a country where he had never been. Lead children in talking about trust in God.

Because Columbus was Italian, serve an Italian dinner. Use world maps as place mats, and a toy boat for a centerpiece.

United Nations Day. Serve an international dinner—first course from one country, main course from another, and so on. Decorate your table with flags from many nations.

Talk about how the United Nations was born. Discuss the Scripture verse displayed in the lobby of the UN headquarters: ". . . they shall beat their swords into plowshares, and their spears into pruning hooks; nation shall not lift up sword against nation, neither shall they learn war any more" (Isa. 2:4 RSV).

Time Change Day. Because everyone can sleep an hour later on Sunday morning when the time changes in the fall, let the children stay up an hour longer on Saturday night and do something together in that extra hour. Read a story, have a pillow fight, go out for hot chocolate, or make popcorn. Talk about time as God's gift to us and how we need to make the best use of our time. (That includes taking time for fun with our kids.)

Substitute a harvest festival for Halloween.

Halloween. When our children were little, not much thought was given to the occult aspect of Halloween. It was simply a fun night for the kids to dress up in costumes and go to the neighbors' houses. But today parents need to give serious thought to this holiday. With so much occult activity and satanic worship in our country and others, we need to be very careful not to open the door to any of this.

And yet the neighbors' kids are celebrating and yours will feel bad if they can't. Substitute other activities and do them with so much style that your kids will never notice they are not celebrating like everyone else. Have an All Saints party where children dress up like a Bible character. Have a harvest festival and visit a pumpkin farm. Eat pumpkin ice cream afterward. Take your kids to the store the day after Halloween and let them buy a generous supply of candy, which will be available at a discounted price.

November

Election Day. Have a red, white, and blue theme at the dinner table. Talk about the responsibility of American citizens to vote. Talk about the relationship between being a good citizen and a good Christian.

Veterans Day. Fly your American flag again today. Talk about the purpose of this day. Research some great American heroes and talk about what they did for this country. Discuss people in your family who are veterans. Or better still, if possible, invite those people to come and share their experiences with your children.

December

Bill of Rights Day. Did you know that such a day exists? The Bill of Rights of the American Constitution is probably the most important document of its kind ever formulated. If your children are old enough, read the Bill of Rights and tell them why each point is important. Give them the Christian perspective on each point.

Winter. Have a winter festival. Let your children cut paper snowflakes from tissue paper and post them all over your windows. Let them buy a new winter hat or mittens. Make popcorn balls to look like snowballs or pop some corn and string it in preparation for Christmas. Talk about this being the shortest day of the year. Explain how short the days are in places like Alaska and Lapland, which are nearer the Arctic Circle. Get out a seed catalog and discuss what you will plant when it is spring.

That takes us through the year with dozens of ideas for celebrating everything on the calendar. There are still more reasons to celebrate:

Birthdays—Make the birthday person feel special.
First day of school
Last day of school
Anniversaries—parents, grandparents
Graduation—fly a banner for the one graduating
Special awards won by family members
Favorite team wins
A special purchase—such as a new car
Leaving home—going away for camp, college
Coming home again

Life is so short, and the time we have with our children is even shorter. Why shouldn't it be fun to be together? Why shouldn't we celebrate everything? In doing so, we may find we are celebrating life itself.

5

Family Seasoning

Holidays

Christmas

Is there a man, woman, boy, or girl alive who does not love Christmas? And yet Christmas can be a time of extreme stress if parents do not slow down and enjoy their children and their home during this season. Do everything you can to keep a calm atmosphere that honors Christ throughout the holidays.

We talked in the previous chapter about the importance of establishing your own traditions in your own home. This is vitally important at Christmas. Take time at Christmas to share your belief that God gave his Son, Jesus, to be our Savior.

There are dozens of ways to make Jesus the focal point of Christmas celebrations. One way is to have a birthday party for Jesus. Even the smallest toddlers can relate to a birthday party. It was always a fun thing to do at our house.

We decorated a cake together and put birthday candles on it. On Christmas day we sang happy birthday to Jesus, blew out the candles, and ate the cake. I don't remember ever being asked how Jesus was going to get his piece of cake.

Advent Season

Observing the season of Advent, which begins the Sunday after Thanksgiving, is another way to focus on the true meaning of Christmas. For this observance you'll need an Advent wreath with five candles. You can purchase them at church supply stores or make your own by inserting candles into a Styrofoam circle that has been covered with sprigs of evergreen or holly. (Remember, never leave burning candles unattended and replace those that burn down close to the wreath.)

If you construct your own advent wreath, make it a family holiday project. Send everyone out to search for greens or let them help purchase some from a store. There are many opinions about the proper color of the Advent candles. Some use four red ones around the outside and a white one in the middle. Others use pink candles around the outside and a purple one in the middle. But the color really doesn't matter.

There are also different teachings about the significance of each candle. One interpretation is the first candle represents the prophets who foretold Christ's birth; the second represents Mary, the mother of Christ; the third represents Joseph; the fourth, the shepherds; and the one in the middle represents Christ. Your Christian bookstore will have booklets giving directions for short celebrations for Advent.

An Advent Celebration

First Week: Prophecy Candle

It is important that your children know Christ's birth was prophesied long before he came. His coming was planned by God from the beginning of all things. Here is a partial list of Scriptures that prophesied his coming:

Genesis 3:15
Isaiah 7:14
Isaiah 9:1–2, 6–7
Isaiah 52:13–53:12
Malachi 3:1

Read several of these Scriptures together, and talk about what you have read. Then one person should light the first candle. Sing a Christmas carol or two. Then blow out the candle and leave the wreath where the whole family can see it.

Second Week: Mary Candle

The second candle is for Mary, the mother of Jesus. Read together the story of Gabriel's announcement to her in Luke 1:26–38. Help your children understand that Mary was being given the highest honor any woman could ever have—to become the mother of the Savior of the world.

Light the prophecy candle again and have a second family member light the candle for Mary. Then sing appropriate Christmas carols.

The story of Gabriel's announcement would be a good one for the family to dramatize. Put on bathrobes and towels for head coverings. Let one person be the angel who announced the good news to Mary.

Talk about what happened to Mary. Why did the angel tell her not to be afraid? How do family members think Mary felt? Why was Mary so willing to become the mother of Jesus? If your children are old enough, talk abut the stigma attached to this event. Explain that Mary, although engaged, was not yet married. Explain what that would mean in her culture. Pray together and thank God for sending Jesus.

Third Week: Joseph Candle

The third candle represents Joseph. Read Matthew 1:18–25 in which Joseph is told about Jesus' birth.

Have family members relight the first two candles and then have a third family member light the Joseph candle. Sing appropriate carols. Once again, family members could act out the story.

Discuss how Joseph must have felt when he saw the angel. Be sure your children understand that Joseph was the earthly father of Jesus and that God entrusted Mary and Jesus into his hands, but God is the heavenly Father of Jesus. You will have to tailor this discussion to the ages of your children.

Fourth Week: Shepherds Candle

Read Luke 2:8–20, the story of the angel's pronouncement to the shepherds in the fields.

Relight the first three candles. (You may have to replace some of them by now.) Sing appropriate Christmas carols.

Talk together about why the shepherds were in the fields. Emphasize that they were the first to greet the new baby lying in a manger. Discuss their humble attitude, our attitude toward Jesus, and the importance of adoring Jesus Christ.

Spend time together praying. Encourage the children to make statements of adoration to Christ.

Christmas Day

Read the passage about the birth of Christ in Luke 2:1–7.

Relight all four candles and then lift them from their places. Together as a family, light the center candle, which represents Christ. Reinsert the other candles in their places. Sing Christmas carols together and rejoice that Christ is born.

Pray together and give thanks for God's great gift, Jesus Christ. Let the candles burn throughout dinner if you are doing your Advent celebration along with a meal. If not, put the wreath in a safe place and let the candles burn for a time.

Another Advent Idea

Some families celebrate Advent with a Bible reading program similar to the one listed above, but instead of using candles they use a nativity scene.

The first week the empty manger is placed in a prominent position—low enough so the littlest ones can see it. The idea is to move the figures toward the manger scene a little each week. The first week (prophecy) use no figures because prophecy is foretelling something no one has seen yet. Read the same Scriptures and talk about prophecy in general. Talk about the people who waited and waited for the Messiah.

The second week place Mary somewhere in the room, but not at the manger. Place an angel nearby when you read the story of the announcement. Use the same carols and readings.

The third week place Joseph near Mary and the angel figure nearby. Read the Scriptures relating to Joseph and the angel's announcement to him. Sing the appropriate carols and pray together.

The fourth week read and talk about Joseph and Mary's journey to Bethlehem. Let the children move the figures closer and closer to the manger through the devotional time. Then finally place them by the manger.

On Christmas Day let the children place the Christ child in the manger. Read the appropriate Scriptures and sing carols. Then place the shepherds somewhere in the room and bring the angel figures to make their announcement. After this, bring the shepherds into the scene as well. If you have time, read the Scriptures given above.

Reserve the wise men for Epiphany, which is described next.

Epiphany

Epiphany, celebrated on January 6, is the traditional holiday that celebrates the revealing of Christ to the Gentiles, represented by the wise men from the east. In some countries this is the day for giving gifts. In many places it is considered the conclusion of the Christmas season.

Our family celebrated Epiphany a few times by leaving our Christmas tree up until this day. In the evening we gathered together and read all the Christmas cards we had received during the holidays. Sometimes we had been too busy to read them carefully. We chose the cards we considered the prettiest, the funniest, the most meaningful, and so on.

We usually played our favorite Christmas records once again before putting them away for the year. And we ate the leftover Christmas goodies during the evening.

It is a lovely way to conclude the Christmas season. The next morning I took down the tree and packed everything related to Christmas.

If you used nativity figures to celebrate Advent, read the Scriptures relating to the wise men. As you read, move the figures closer and closer to the nativity scene. You will have to explain to the children that the wise men probably did not come to Bethlehem until as much as two years after Christ was born. And as far as singing, what else could you sing but "We Three Kings of Orient Are"?

Easter

Perhaps the most important holiday of the year for a Christian family is Easter. Without the resurrection we have no hope and no future. But because Christ lives, we can face the future. In a war-infested, poverty-ridden, disease-suffering world, our children need hope.

Easter can be a shared experience through which we emphasize again and again the importance of our relationship with God. We value Jesus Christ. We value the cross and the finished work of Calvary. We need to pass those values on to our children.

Sometime during the holiday, sit down together and read the Easter story. If the children are able to read, let them participate. If they are unable to read, choose a Bible storybook that is simple enough for them to understand. As you share this reading time together, remember that the story you are reading is the most important one in the Bible—the most important one in all of history. Take time for it.

Here are some other ideas for Easter observances:

Color eggs. Most children love coloring Easter eggs. Do it as a family and be creative. You may want to hide the eggs on Easter afternoon and let the kids hunt for them.

On Easter Sunday, after church and dinner, we played in the yard with the kids and hid the eggs everywhere. We had a shaggy gray poodle that often gave away the hiding places. The children never tired of having us hide the eggs or of hiding them themselves. It was a fun time of shared experience for our family. We weren't trying to communicate any heavy messages. We were just playing with our kids.

Easter baskets. Many parents enjoy filling Easter baskets with candy and small toys for their children.

Easter lilies. In our church, families buy Easter lilies in memory of loved ones. The flowers remain in the church through the Easter celebration and then are taken home. Perhaps you could make it a family project to buy an Easter lily for your church in memory of someone you love.

Thanksgiving Day

A little more than three hundred years ago our forefathers stood on the shores of a new land and gave thanks to God for keeping them through the previous year.

Consider all that has happened in the three hundred years since then. Today our land is teeming with people, industry, health facilities, automobiles, homes, and thousands of wonderful things. We have much for which to thank God. We should value God's good gifts to us in America and we should teach our children to value them as well. Thanksgiving is a time to do that.

Review the story of the Pilgrims by getting a storybook from the library. Or perhaps your children will be able to tell you much about the holiday because they have studied it in school. Let them share with you.

A delightful film available in video is *An American Tail*, which tells the story of a Russian mouse family that immigrates to America. At one point all the mice are pouring onto Ellis Island. In the background a song can be heard with the words that are engraved on the Statue of Liberty:

> Give me your tired, your poor,
> Your huddled masses yearning to breathe free,
> The wretched refuse of your teeming shore,
> Send these, the homeless, tempest-tost, to me,
> I lift my lamp beside the golden door!
>
> **Emma Lazarus**

Although it is a fantasy story and is not about people, it may help your children understand what it was like for people to come to this county from poverty, oppression, and fear. Talk about it and lead them in giving thanks.

Many churches and civic organizations have programs not only for contributing to needy families, but also for cooking dinner for these people. What a learning experience it would be for your children if they could stand beside you while you work at a shelter, helping feed the hungry. They will know instantly that you value people and because you do, you are giving back some of your life and time to those who are less fortunate.

Thanksgiving should be a time for sharing. Look around your community to find lonely people—singles with or without children—and invite them in to share the day. Every person who sits at your table brings a new insight about life.

Whatever you do, make giving thanks a part of your celebration. If your church has a Thanksgiving Day service, attend it with your children. Talk afterward about how to give thanks to God. Pray together and, by your example, teach your children to offer prayers of thanksgiving to God.

The well-seasoned family is a joyful family celebrating the important holidays in a way that pleases God because it puts the emphasis where it belongs—on him.

6

A Night
on the Town

In some families children grow up without ever going to see even one art show or traveling exhibit because it is not something their parents value. That's all right. Each family has a different value system. Different is not wrong; it's just different. Many families value sporting events above cultural events. That's all right too. But being exposed to cultural events stretches our children and gives them a broader view of the world. It is something worth considering when deciding how your family's limited entertainment budget will be spent.

Any metropolitan area offers more cultural events than you can possibly find time to attend. Even if you do not live in a metropolitan area, you can still find some cultural events.

I grew up in a very small town in Montana where the only cultural center, if you could call it that, was the local theater. But Butte was just thirty-five miles away, and there I was able to attend some cultural events. I heard Yehudi Menuhin playing violin in concert. Afterward my violin teacher took me backstage to meet him. I've never forgotten the thrill of that moment.

Whenever our school music department showed films of operas and ballet, I sat entranced. I often listened to the Metropolitan Opera on radio on Saturdays while helping with housework. Even though I lived in a town of 4,500 people high in the mountains of Montana, and even though it was thirty-five miles to the nearest town, which also had little to offer culturally, it was possible to learn about and appreciate the arts simply by taking advantage of what *was* available.

Look around you if you are isolated in some small town and see what is available. Often the cultural events in rural America are centered around the ethnic group that established the town. Some wonderful traditions are handed down from generation to generation. Find out about them and begin to learn from your neighbors.

Some cultural events are expensive, but if you look at them as an investment—an investment you cannot lose—then the price tag doesn't seem quite so high. It is a matter of priorities. Better to have one really spectacular event in the children's growing-up years than dozens of trips to McDonald's.

With the advent of video, it is possible to bring into our homes some of the best cultural events in the world. It is simply a matter of choosing to see those videos rather than a steady diet of Walt Disney movies.

Some Cultural Events to Consider

Ballet. Some people consider ballet a feminine interest. It is a beautiful art form often performed in soft, exquisite, flowing costumes. But it is more than that. It is also athletic ability at its finest. Dancers must be conditioned to a level of Olympic readiness. The leaps, lifts, spins, and stretches of the dance are truly athletic achievements.

Several ballets are classics, and since you probably will not be going on a regular basis, why not choose those? I already have mentioned *The Nutcracker* ballet. Another great classic is *Swan Lake*. It will help your children understand what is happening if they know the plot of the story. Do a little research ahead of time, and explain to them what is happening.

Opera. Opera is another art form that is not understood by many people because few ever take the time to find out about it. Opera, as you probably know, is a dramatic play that is sung rather than spoken.

Because so many operas are performed in languages other than English, they are impossible to understand for those who speak only English. If you want to go to an opera that is sung in a language other than English, you will have to do some studying about the opera ahead of time. Whether it's in English or not, it still is a good idea to learn the opera's plot.

Plays. Attending a first-rate production of a play is usually expensive. But if you have an opportunity, it is certainly worth taking the family occasionally. Less expensive theater is often available as well. Children's theater is often a good choice. You'll see some very creative portrayals of well-known children's stories.

Many times when we were traveling, we discovered theater in the park. Fort Worth, Texas, has a fine Shakespearean theater in a park every week throughout the summer and it's free. Just get there early to find a good place to sit on the grass.

Once in Montana, in a town even smaller than my hometown, we encountered theater produced by university students in the local park. We saw *Cyrano de Bergerac.* The creative set changes alone made the production worthwhile.

A word of warning. Be very careful about live theater. Know what you will be seeing and try to find out how it will be interpreted. We had seen quite a bit of Shakespeare before we went to an outdoor presentation in our city. The way in which the actors were portraying this particular play—a comedy—was so lewd that we decided this was not for us, and we left.

In our city there is also a fine Christian drama group that we have seen perform a number of times. It was they who introduced our family to C. S. Lewis's *The Lion, the Witch and the Wardrobe.*

You also may find a reader's theater in your area. This is theater in which actors sitting on stools read the play with such expression and style that you may be convinced you are seeing the action. It shows what can be done with the voice alone.

Symphony. We need to introduce a love of good music to our children. When our children were infants and I put them down for naps, I often turned on a classical music radio station to cover neighborhood noises. When a youngster has been exposed to good music, even though she may for a time find an interest in rock music, she won't forget the good music. It cannot be taken away from her.

Take your kids to the symphony when there will be music they can enjoy. Modern symphony orchestras are becoming very creative. Sometimes there are laser light shows to accompany the orchestra or whole evenings when themes from movies are the symphony's fare. If the Boston Pops orchestra ever comes to your area, do everything you can to hear it. The Boston Pops will delight you *and* your children.

Take your kids to the symphony.

When you go to your local symphony, try to take the kids backstage to meet the conductor or some of the musicians. It will make an indelible impression on them. Who knows? Perhaps there is a budding concert musician at your house.

In some cities concerts are held in local parks. Here in our city the symphony orchestra presents a series of summer concerts called brown-bag concerts, which usually take place at noon in a downtown park. Everyone brings a lunch and listens.

Traveling exhibits. King Tut was a favorite traveling exhibit for our family, but there have been other notable exhibits as well. Let me mention some of them.

One memorable exhibit was a collection of eggs that had been handcrafted by the Fabergé family for the czar of Russia as gifts to family members. They are exquisite. Some have little doors that open to tiny scenes. One has a huge emerald set at the top. Others have miniature scenes in complete detail painted all around the egg.

Another display at the local art museum was the gold of the Incas. We often think of the Incan culture as being very primitive, but a look at these golden treasures would convince you otherwise. Among the treasures was fabric of an intricate design that was shot through with golden threads.

The tall ships are worth seeing. They travel from port to port around the country. These huge sailing vessels all rigged and moving out to sea are spectacular.

During the bicentennial celebration, the Constitution of the United States made a tour across the country. Another time there was a full display of medieval armor, featuring pieces of armor used at different times in history. The Son of Heaven exhibit from China has been on display. The display shows clay figures removed from a grave in China. There was also a working display of Chinese crafts exhibited in our city. There was everything from papermaking to silk tapestry weaving on a gigantic ancient loom.

Universities and colleges often have traveling exhibits available to the public. It was at our local university that we saw some well-known Leonardo da Vinci paintings and sketches.

Watch your newspaper for information about these traveling exhibits. Call local museums, art galleries, and ticket offices to see what is being planned for your area.

Other Fun Nights Out

Dinner out. If it is at all possible to squeeze it into your budget, take your kids out to eat occasionally in nice places. Teach them which fork to use and when. Then later in their life when they are confronted by an array of silver, they will not be intimidated or ill at ease. Your job is to give them the skills they will need when they leave you, and among the skills they need to learn are social skills.

Eating out can be an ethnic adventure. We've eaten borscht in a Russian restaurant, true East Indian food, and, of course, Mexican food dozens of times. We've also wandered into English tea shops at high tea time. What a delightful experience!

Be bold and see what eating adventures you can discover. In doing so, you are exposing your children to a broader view of life and are creating patterns of interest that will expand them as people. You too will grow as a person as you share these adventures with your children.

Sporting events. Almost every village and town in the nation has some kind of sporting event going on most of the year. In the fall it may be high school football; in winter, basketball; in spring, baseball. Larger cities have professional teams playing the same sports as well as hockey, soccer, and a host of others.

But other events are worth considering. We took our kids to the national ice skating championships. We had watched some of the performers on television for years. What a thrill it was to see them zoom up to the end of the rink and look right up at us! What a joy to see the grace, the form, and the athletic prowess of the skaters! After that it was easy to discuss with our kids having a vision in life and working to fulfill that goal, knowing full well that it may cost you dearly.

There are local swim meets to attend. Swim meets are noisy, fun events. There's the starting gun going off, the splash as the participants hit the water, the water flying from arms and feet, the touch, and the finish. Of course, swim meets are even more fun when someone you know is participating.

Circus. Every few years take the kids to the circus if you possibly can. The circus is pure hype and fun. There is so much going on at a circus that you will enjoy watching your little one's head turn and her eyes light up with wonder.

A fun thing to do in conjunction with the circus is to go an hour or so before the performance and ask the circus personnel if you can walk through the area where the caged animals are kept. Sometimes you can get very close, and your little ones can get a good look at lions, tigers, and elephants. If you hang around long enough you may see the elephants dressed for their performance. There are all kinds of interesting people running around backstage at a circus. As I said, it is great fun.

A night on the town can be lots of fun for a family, but the greatest value is derived from just being together and sharing new adventures. Being with your children, talking about what you are doing and seeing, and sharing your life and your values with them is vitally important. Think about how you can have a night on the town with your kids.

7

The Ultimate Adventure

The Family Vacation

An annual vacation of some kind is an absolute necessity for a busy family. It is essential that we get away from responsibilities, telephones, and schedules sometime during the year. It's a wonderful time to spend together as a family, getting to know our kids better, finding out what is going on in their heads, and teaching values. There are plenty of opportunities during a two- to three-week vacation for teaching values.

Vacation time can also be a time of great stress for some families. Most families are not used to being shut up together in a car for hours on end. Someone once said, "There are two ways to travel—first class and with kids." Spending twenty-four hours a day with your kids is very different, especially for dads, from the usual routine—a quick bedtime story, a prayer, and a good-night kiss.

Some of the stress related to vacationing can be avoided by advance thinking and planning. One thing we can do is to *reduce expectations of what the vacation should be*. We need to learn to relax and just take it as it comes. Who says we have to make seven hundred miles a day? This is supposed to be a vacation, and believe it or not, getting there can be half the fun if we slow down and enjoy it.

Planning ahead can help to reduce stress. Nothing is worse than a car of tired, hungry, cranky kids (and parents) who have nowhere to spend the night. Have you ever pulled into a town late at night and found the annual rodeo has filled every bed for miles? We did. There's nothing to do but hit the road and keep driving until you find someplace to stay. And in Montana that could be a hundred or more miles.

Planning and flexibility reduce stress on vacations.

Continually spending more money than you had planned greatly increases stress. Vacationing isn't much fun for the bill payer when that person realizes what is going to happen once the family returns home. Try to discover some free things you can do along the way. Some planning, such as writing to travel bureaus, will help you locate those places that offer free activities.

To reduce stress in the car, plan activities to do while driving. Be sure to provide each child with small books, toys, puzzles, or coloring books he has chosen. Sleep is a very good thing for little people to do when traveling. Bring along favorite pillows, stuffed animals, and blankets.

Take frequent breaks on driving vacations. We found that everything went better for us if we avoided restaurants (more sitting) and ate at least some of our meals in a park or even at a roadside rest area. A fast, hard game of tag or Frisbee helps to get rid of a lot of pent-up energy. Let the kids run off their energy to their heart's content.

Expect some problems. Problems abound when you are traveling. There can be car problems, kids can get sick in cars, motel reservations can get twisted up, and the attractions you wanted to see can cost too much. Try to stay flexible and see what creative solutions you can find to solve those problems. Who knows? You may come up with a better idea than the original plan. Your children will learn about problem solving as they watch you cope with problems on your family's vacation trip.

Consider the ages of your children when planning your vacation. Small children are just as happy with a short trip to a beach or lake as they would be with a trip to Disney World.

Don't be afraid to travel with very young children. Recently I witnessed some truly creative mothering at O'Hare International Airport in Chicago. A very young mother was seated cross-legged on the floor. Near her a large bag was open at the top. From this she handed food to a bouncing toddler. Lying on a folded blanket on the floor in front of her was a four-month-old infant.

Suddenly I realized the air around them was filled with bubbles. She was blowing soap bubbles to the delight of her two youngsters. We, the rest of the passengers in the waiting area, watched with interest as the baby kicked and cooed and followed the bubbles with his eyes. The toddler was bouncing around and trying to burst as many of the bubbles as possible. This clever, young mother turned what could have been a tiring and difficult situation into a time of sharing and joy.

Traveling with young children does demand creativity on the parents' part. It also demands that we keep everything simple. Start with simple family vacations and make them increasingly more appealing to growing kids and finally to teenagers merely by planning bigger and better events.

Where to Go

Where to go is probably best determined by how much money you have available for traveling expenses. It takes lots of money to fly a family to a foreign destination. It takes a considerable sum of money to put a family up in a luxury hotel at a theme park, unless you can find a great travel package. It takes a lot of money to spend several weeks on the road, traveling across the United States. But there are ways to have a great but inexpensive vacation.

If your children are small, pick a place for vacation with lots of sunshine and some water, preferably near home. Maybe you can rent a cottage at a lake or oceanside. Many of these cottages are fully equipped, so all you have to bring are your clothes and play equipment. Most have kitchens, and since families have to eat even if they stay at home, the cost of meals is not an added expense.

If a family is economizing by doing their own cooking, it is important that all able-bodied people get involved in the cooking and cleanup. *Mom needs a vacation too!* Perhaps to ease the strain of cooking, some meals can be eaten out, depending on your budget.

This simple arrangement works well for small children. Drive somewhere less than two hours away from where you live. Set up a homelike atmosphere and schedule. Put the children to bed at about the usual time. (The first night might be tough because of their being in a new place.) Get up at about the usual time. Eat the same food that you eat at home, to avoid crankiness and upset stomachs.

The big difference should be that you and the child can go out to the water and throw rocks or splash about. You can search for rocks and shells and interesting bugs, or an unusual leaf or stick. You can read stories while sitting in the sunshine, or if it rains, you can stay inside and watch the rain through the window, sit by a fire, or play games together.

Together is the key word here. Whether Dad and the boys are washing dishes after a meal or Mom and the girls are riding mopeds down the beach, the key is being and doing things *together.*

If your family is ready for popular tourist areas, go in the off-season and save big bucks. The summer months are off-season in Florida, home of Disney World. Summer is also off-season for well-known ski areas. Check out Snowbird, Utah; Sun Valley, Idaho; and other popular ski areas all over the country.

Swap your home with another family through a home-exchange program. Some people find this an exciting way to see a new area of the country without the cost of hotels. There are exchanges available in Hawaii and even internationally. Contact Home Link, 800-638-3841, for more information.

National parks offer inexpensive places to stay. Many of our national parks have wonderful old hotels and lodges that are relatively inexpensive. Because they are old, sometimes the accommodations are also dated. I remember that at Old Faithful Lodge in Yellowstone Park, it was necessary to go down the hall to the bathroom. But the place had charm and was inexpensive, which made up for the inconvenience. The lodge also had rooms with full accommodations at higher prices. National parks also have woodsy cabins, teepees, luxurious hotels, and campgrounds—something for every taste.

Think about tent cabins. Some national parks (Yosemite, for one) have a trail-hiking system that includes tent cabins and tent restaurants set up at intervals along the trail. You can hike five to ten miles and have a place to stay and eat without carrying any equipment. The full length of the trail is about fifty miles.

State parks also offer inexpensive lodging. The Oregon state park system is one of the finest in the country. Each ocean campsite offers something in addition to the ocean, beach, and campsites. Usually there is a naturalist who presents a nightly program. There are visitors' centers and interpretive displays set up in many of the state parks.

National and state parks offer inexpensive lodging and recreation.

There are some families who have an "always" place. Sometimes it's a family cottage where they go to escape the rigors of life and be with members of the extended family. Sometimes it's a certain vacation destination—a certain cottage, a certain suite in a certain hotel, a certain campground. There is a stability to that kind of vacationing that may be right for your family.

A recreational vehicle may be the answer for your family. Friends who have vacationed in recreational vehicles for years tell me it's the only way to go. That may be true. A recreational vehicle will give you great mobility and variety in where you can stay.

Recreational vehicles are another way to give children a sense of stability while traveling. They sleep in the same bed every night, hang their clothes on the same hooks every day, and eat their meals at the same table, even though the vehicle may be parked in a different spot every night. This kind of routine avoids a lot of upset and confusion in their lives.

If you don't think you would use a recreational vehicle enough to warrant owning one, you can rent one. They come in all price ranges, from simple to luxury versions. Remember that recreational vehicles consume a huge amount of gasoline, so figure that cost into your vacation budget as well.

One word of caution. Because so many of us choose to live far away from our parents and families, we often think vacation time means a visit to the grandparents' house. It's important for

your children to know their grandparents and be able to benefit from the influence of their lives and experience. It's important that children get a sense of their history from their grandparents. But what often happens when parents and grandparents
get together is that children are left out of the conversations. It
is important from time to time to include your children in the
conversation. Bring it down to their level. It's important to
arrange your schedule so each child has one-on-one time with
each of the grandparents.

When your children are older, extend your vacation plans. If
they are old enough to hike, you can plan day hiking, city walking, backpacking trips, or other walking activities. There is no
better way to see what's there than to get out and walk.

Set Goals for Family Travel

Whatever your goal for a family vacation, you can accomplish
it by working together to achieve it. Part of the fun is in the planning and in the saving together to make it happen.

You'll never know what you can do together as a family until
you set some goals. There's nothing wrong with children contributing some of their earnings to make a family vacation happen. There's nothing wrong with having a garage sale and getting rid of excess possessions to make it happen. There's nothing
wrong with someone getting a part-time job or setting up a cottage industry to make a special family vacation a possibility. In
fact those times when everyone has worked together to make a
special trip come about may be more memorable than when Dad
shells out all the money for the trip.

Start building a file of places your family would like to go.
Each year, usually in the spring, the popular supermarket magazines have articles about family travel. Clip those and file them
for future reference or purchase a travel magazine and look at
the little ads in the back. You'll find ordering information for
brochures and maps—more information than you can ever use.
Most of it is free. If they're old enough, let the kids send for the
information. They'll learn how to do research, have fun getting

the mail, and be involved in the planning process, which will make the vacation very special to them.

In tight economic years, it may be hard to justify including a family vacation in your budget. But it may be more important at this time than ever for your family to get away from the day-to-day stress of trying to make ends meet. Your family may be desperately in need of time for rebuilding emotional ties to one another. In those years, take an inexpensive vacation, planning and budgeting carefully so you don't add to the stress by overspending.

Packing for a Trip

Always strive to take less. When you have a small child, that is almost impossible. Whether it's a bassinet or a portable crib, a baby buggy or a stroller, a potty-chair or a half-ton of diapers—or all of the above—you get the feeling you are carrying an entire nursery in your car.

During this period, I learned to take as little as possible for myself. Now I can take a three-week overseas trip with one small backpack and a camera bag. I could travel for three months with the same amount of equipment, although I might have to buy something along the way to keep me from going mad from wearing the same three sets of clothes.

Here are some general tips for cutting down on the amount of stuff you take on a trip. Wear your heaviest clothes—a suit or other two-piece outfit. Make sure the pieces of the suit coordinate with everything else you are taking. The jacket should coordinate with other slacks or skirts. The skirt or pants should mix with sweaters, shirts, or blouses. Carry a lightweight raincoat; one with a zip-out lining is best. The raincoat can double as a bathrobe, if need be.

In selecting a wardrobe for a trip, I always base everything on one color. If the basic is a black skirt or slacks, then all tops and jackets coordinate with that black skirt. One of my favorite color combinations, because I never tire of it, is red, white, and blue. It always seems fresh to me. I want my wardrobe so well coordinated that I can reach for any top and any bottom in the suitcase (in the dark) and know they go together.

Take two other skirts, slacks, or jeans in dark colors, to cut down on washing. Take two or three lightweight (easy to dry) tops, then add a lightweight wool sweater.

Be sure you have a good pair of walking shoes that are well broken in and comfortable. Take one pair of dress shoes and a pair of sandals that can triple as beach shoes, slippers, and casual street shoes.

Take about three or four changes of underwear, socks, and panty hose for each person in the family. Add some kind of sleepwear for each person. When our two children were teenagers, they were most comfortable sleeping in a T-shirt and shorts. Be sure to take a clothesline and pins, so you can wash out your clothing.

More can be put in less space if you roll clothing, especially cotton knits, undergarments, and sleepwear. Fold clothing items smoothly and then roll them up.

Keep cosmetics and toiletry items to a minimum. Decide on just one set of makeup and use it with all outifts. Repack all toiletries in unbreakable, lightweight plastic bottles.

Take along some basic first-aid supplies. I usually take along adhesive bandages, antiseptic ointment, antidiarrheal medication, laxatives, aspirin, vitamins, motion sickness medication (if appropriate), and any daily medications. Beyond that, you can stop at a drugstore or see a doctor.

Let's Go Camping

Many American families with young children have discovered the joys and agonies of camping vacations. One thing for sure: Once your equipment is purchased, camping is probably one of the least expensive of all vacations. If you refrain from taking along more than you actually need, you can probably get by with hauling the equipment in a car-top carrier or even in the trunk of your car.

Campgrounds in all fifty states are plentiful. Some are commercial but many are in state or national parks and most have water, electrical hookups, hot showers, and other amenities to make you forget you're camping.

Since national and state parks are so popular, make reservations several months in advance of your intended vacation time.

If I have expertise in any kind of inexpensive family vacationing, it is in the area of camping. I've done it most of my life. Sometimes I've loved it. (Who wouldn't love stepping out of a tent on a crisp early morning to find a deer browsing in the meadow nearby and the sun just beginning to touch a snow-capped mountain?) Sometimes I've hated it. (Who wouldn't hate it when hail pounds the top of the tent and it begins to leak and you go out in the night to investigate what's happening and step into six inches of ice-cold water and mud?) I'm the world's laziest tent camper. I also love my comfort. Tent camping, comfort, and laziness *can* all go together.

I do believe that camping provides great training in problem solving. It introduces so many problems that the whole process makes children grow into young adults who are able to cope in almost every travel situation.

Meals

While our family was camping, I always made it a policy to eat the same kind of food we ate at home. Picnic food is all right for one meal, but on an extended vacation, it can cause all kinds of problems. Instead of a constant diet of potato salad, baked beans, hot dogs, potato chips, and pickles, we ate what we normally ate at the dinner table at home. Early in our camping experience we invested in a good propane stove and a good-size tank for the propane. The stove folded up to the size of a briefcase, and a tank of propane would last through a vacation.

I got so I could set up the stove and have a meal ready to eat in twenty to thirty minutes. I've cooked not only in campgrounds, but in roadside rest areas, city parks, and almost every other place I could find a flat surface to set up the stove.

I usually tried to stop at a grocery store and buy fresh meat late in the afternoon for the evening meal. (This is also a good time to replenish the ice supply in the cooler.) We would eat the meat either by itself, if it was steak or meat patties, or incorporate it into a one-dish skillet meal. The meal was filled out with salad or fresh fruit, cooked vegetables, and a simple dessert. I always had a backup meat ready—such as canned chicken—in case we couldn't get to a store.

Breakfasts were made up of some combination of cold cereal, pancakes, omelettes, or scrambled eggs. While I made breakfast, I also made lunch and packed it in a backpack. Anything that might spoil was kept in an ice chest and taken out when needed. By fixing lunch at the same time I fixed breakfast, I was through with food preparation until the evening meal—and that took only about thirty minutes.

Before going camping, watch for sales on prepackaged food.

To further aid my laziness, I used paper plates tucked into rattan plate holders. I prefer real silverware to plastic, so we used stainless steel knives, forks, and spoons. This also made cleanup easy, because as soon as a meal was cooked, I put two enamel pans of water on the camp stove and then heated the water to wash the dishes. It was easy to plunk the silver, glasses, and cups right into the hot water, give them a quick wash and rinse, and spread them out on a towel to air-dry. Some campers put everything in a net bag and hang it on a tree or tent pole to dry.

I stored silverware in one of those tubes potato chips come in. It was just the right size. I also found it was easier to find the implement you were looking for if forks and knives were stored point down and spoons were stored bowl up. Other implements for cooking were very few (see the list at the end of this chapter).

You can save on food for camping trips by planning ahead and watching for sales on prepackaged items. Any kind of packaged pasta or noodle dish can be mixed with a number of different meats for a quick meal. Buy canned whole chicken for a chicken and dumpling dinner or for chicken and noodles. Buy small hams in cans and other canned meats.

For one summer's camping I bought, on sale, individual hot-chocolate-mix packets, premeasured packages of orange breakfast drink, one-serving packets of mashed potatoes, a hot syrup mix, dry milk in one-quart packets, and iced tea mix in premeasured packets.

To save storage space, remove all the ingredients from each box and repackage them in plastic bags. Be sure to include the cooking instructions from the box.

I like to prepackage all the ingredients of a meal into one bag. For example: Put a noodle dinner in a small plastic bag, then put that bag in a larger one, along with a can of boned chicken, tuna, or salmon. Put in a can of vegetables or freeze-dried vegetables, available from almost any outdoor supply store. You might even include drink mixes and tea bags. Label the bag with the day you intend to use it. You don't even have to think about what to eat on a particular night of a camping trip. What could be easier?

Let your kids get involved with meal planning and prepackaging of food. It will be great training for them. They can help cook it at the campsite too if they're old enough.

Since a vacation is supposed to be a time to free your mind, I like to plan my menus ahead of time, on cards. When it's time to pack the food, it is easy to make sure I have everything I need. It's very freeing to know dinner is planned and all the ingredients are together.

Whether you are camping or economizing by cooking some of your meals on a long driving trip, remember that there may be long days when you will be too tired to cook or bad weather that forces you indoors.

Allow flexibility in your budget, your time, and your attitude for overtired kids and spouses, bad weather, and "I just want to do something different."

Instead of serving desserts with a meal, save them for roadside stops. Look for a fresh fruit stand or a frozen yogurt shop. Try to avoid candy, ice cream, soda pop, and high calorie, high fat chips.

Camping is a wonderful way to save money, but you don't want to be so tight with money that no one has a good time. Plan carefully and spend your money on the activities and adventures you enjoy, like horseback rides around Lake Louise in Canada, taking the aerial tramway to the top of Whistlers' Mountain, seeing extra attractions at Disneyland, or going to a play.

Camping Equipment

Here is a list of the basic equipment needed for a camping trip.

Tent
- poles, stakes
- tent
- axe or hammer for pounding stakes
- ground cloth for under tent

Sleeping Gear
- sleeping bags
- foam pads, rolled up, or air mattresses
- small pillows in dark-colored cases
- air pump, if using air mattresses
- flashlight

Cooking Gear
- stove
- propane tank
- stove lighter
- matches
- ten-inch frying pan
- three nesting cooking pots
- locking pliers
- pancake turner
- large spoon
- vinyl tablecloth
- tongs
- pot holders
- ice chest
- serrated knife
- enamel dishpans
- detergent
- scouring pad
- water container
- thermos
- can opener

Food Staples
- salt and pepper
- small amount of flour
- small amount of sugar
- shortening
- oil
- menu items

Eating
- paper plates
- rattan plate holders
- paper napkins or towels
- thermal cups
- nesting glasses
- silverware
- small plastic bowls with lids

Clothing
- rain gear
- stocking caps
- jackets
- wool sweaters
- swimsuits
- shoes
- personal clothing

Dry Goods

- small rug for the front of tent
- dish towels
- dishcloths
- towels
- washcloths
- soap
- mirror
- first-aid items
- toilet paper with core removed to conserve space

Toiletries

- toothbrushes
- toothpaste
- hair brush
- personal items

Bikes

- bikes
- bike rack
- lock and chain

Fun and Games

- Frisbee
- kite
- games
- books

Family vacations can build wonderful memories. They are well worth the effort, time, and money invested in them to make them work well. They are rich times of sharing yourself, your values, and your love for your kids.

Approach the family vacation with anticipation and expectation that this is going to be a great time for all of you. Plan ahead carefully—and have a wonderful time together!

Family Fun ideas from A to Z

Is your family ready to experience meaningful adventures that your children will remember throughout their life? Here's an abundance of family adventure ideas, but don't stop with these. Dream up your own family adventures.

Airplanes and Airports

An airport is a hubbub of activity. Go to the observation tower and watch planes come and go. Kids love it.

Watch sky divers.

Find a field from which glider planes are towed aloft.

Take the kids for a plane or helicopter ride.

Visit an airplane museum.

Animal Shows

Animal shows are lots of fun for kids. Kids and animals just seem to go together. Talk to owners about their pets.

Local and state fairs are animal shows.

Dressage and other kinds of horse shows are great fun.

Judging livestock for fairs is an interesting procedure to watch.

Many circus events have to do with animals.

Antiques

Children can learn a lot about our history and will feel much closer to those who have lived before us if they can see the implements of work and leisure from earlier eras. An antique store is a good place to expose them to the past. Visit local antique shops and look for unusual items. Talk with the shop owner about the things you see. Find out how they were used in everyday life.

Visit antique shows.

Buy one or two inexpensive items. Old postcards and photos don't cost too much.

Let the child start a collection of some inexpensive type of item—spoons, cards, matchbook covers, and so on. She'll be much more interested in going into an antique shop with you.

Arboretums

Many cities have arboretums with beautiful trees, flowers, walkways, and ponds. Usually there are playground facilities for children and picnic areas as well.

Take a bag of bread to feed the waterfowl.

Take a book to help identify the kinds of birds you may see.

Teach your children to sit quietly observing wildlife and listening to the sound of the trees.

Play games on the lawns.

Wade in the ponds.

Take a book to help you identify the kinds of trees in the arboretum or get a guide from the park's information system. Walk around and talk about the different kinds of trees in the park.

Archaeology

There may be archaeological digs in your area. In many places Native American villages are being unearthed and restored. In some places original cities are being excavated. (The Seattle underground is an example.)

Visit museums that display the findings of archaeological digs.

Attend seminars and classes at museums to learn more about these digs.

Read books about the unearthing of various cultures. The saga of Masada is wonderful reading. The exploration and uncovering of the ancient city of Jericho is also fascinating.

Architecture

Architecture can be a fascinating pursuit. Most American cities have sections of wonderful old houses and buildings. Many of them are trimmed with what I call "gingerbread"— brackets, turnings, rosettes, and shaped shingles.

Find a book on the architecture of your city.

Take architectural walks in your town. Check with the chamber of commerce for information about guided walks or maps.

You may want to collect interesting houses with a camera.

Look for interesting architectural details in new and restored office buildings in your town.

Learn to look up. Much of the architectural detail is above street level.

Give a prize to the one who finds the oldest building during an architectural walk.

Go to the top of some of those interesting office buildings. See if they have a restaurant and at least have dessert there.

Art

Find out how many art galleries your city has. Plan to visit them all.

Try to discover the stories behind the paintings, if at all possible.

Look for the unusual. Modern art can be very amusing.

Look for street art and sculpture. In Seattle there is a statue of a group of individuals and a dog waiting for a bus. It is called *Waiting for the Interurban*. City residents decorate the statue appropriately for the season. They identify with the statue and so give the figures their coats, umbrellas, and so on.

Astronomy

Visit an observatory.

Visit a planetarium.

Buy a telescope and a chart of the stars and start learning about them on your own.

Watch the newspaper and newscasts for unusual planetary alignments, meteor showers, comets, and other unusual heavenly phenomena.

Go someplace where it is really dark, and see how many stars you can see. It may surprise you.

Get books on stars from the library. There are beautiful full-color books that show close-ups of planets, nebulae, galaxies, stars, and other heavenly bodies.

B

Battlefields

There are hundreds, maybe even thousands, of battlefields across our country. These include the sites of Indian massacres, Civil War battles, American Revolutionary War battles, Spanish-American War battles, and others.

Visit battlefields. Walk where history was made.

See sound and light shows often presented at battlefields.

See working dioramas that show the action of the battle.

Tour the museums usually attached to these battlefields and in your mind try to reenact what happened there.

Learn the Gettysburg Address, which was given by President Lincoln at the Gettysburg battlefield.

Beaches

Beaches are wonderful places for families.

Walk or run in the sand.

Fly a kite.

Build a sand castle and let the waves wash it back to sea.

Collect driftwood.

Collect shells, but take them only if it is allowed.

Soak up sunshine.

Swim.

Berry Picking

Learn to identify the kinds of berries that grow in your locale. These may be either domesticated or wild. Take the whole family on a berry picking expedition. Our family could usually pick fifty pounds of strawberries in about forty-five minutes.

Give a prize to the child who picks the most berries, or the biggest berry.

Have a berry feed, inviting all your friends in to help you eat the berries.

Make jam for the whole winter and do it as a family project. It's not difficult and is a project the kids will enjoy.

Bicycling

Bicycling together is a wonderful family activity. It is also good exercise. Even if there are babies in the family, they can be put in carriers on the rear wheel of Mom or Dad's bike or in a bike trailer. I don't think I have ever seen a crying baby on a bicycle. They love it.

Find out where the bike trails are in your area. More and more trails are being developed everywhere in this country. Learn about them through the newspaper, books at your local bookshop, local bike shops, and regional magazines.

Spend a whole day bicycling. Take a picnic lunch to eat along the way or plan to stop at a fun restaurant for lunch.

Go to bicycle races.

Enter your family in a bike-a-thon.

Birds

Go bird-watching.

Buy a bird identification book and try to identify as many birds as possible. Keep a log of the birds you see.

Watch for shows of performing birds.

Boats

There are all kinds of boats and all kinds of activities that take place on the water, from canoeing to hydroplane racing. There is no limit to the adventures boats can provide.

Teach your children water and boating safety; it could save their lives.

Take a canoe trip—either for an afternoon or as part of a camping trip. Slip along the edges of a stream or lake with only the sound of the paddles dipping in and out of the water.

Visit U.S. Navy and Coast Guard ships. Take their tours; you'll all learn a lot.

See a hydroplane race either in person or view it together on television.

Teach your kids to row a boat.

Ride a paddle wheeler.

Visit the *U.S. Constitution* in Boston Harbor.

Try to arrange a visit aboard a tugboat.

Ride a hydrofoil.

Take a speedboat ride.

Learn to water-ski.

Visit research ships.

Take harbor tours and other excursion boat rides.

Botany

There are many adventure ideas that can fit under this rather bookish title. We are surrounded by plants. Our life is dependent on them. We can have a great time together as a family discovering all that there is to know about botany.

Conservatories

Conservatories are wonderful places, especially in the dead of winter. Visiting a conservatory is like stepping out of winter into summer.

Find out if your city has a conservatory.

When you go, try to identify as many flowers and plants as possible.

Some conservatories have live birds or butterflies in them. Watch for them and identify them. They are usually very tame, and it is a good opportunity for your children to see them up close.

Gardening

Gardening can be a family project, one that helps to save money. Gardening can even be done in tubs on a balcony or the patio of an apartment. You don't need much space to have a little salad garden.

Work together to choose a spot for your garden and dig up the soil.

Let the children choose the kind of seeds and plants for the garden—with guidance from you, of course.

Plant, water, and hoe the garden together. Children can learn about hard work and about responsibility by gardening.

There are many spiritual lessons to be learned from a garden. Jesus told many parables that were based on plants and gardening. Talk about these with your children.

Mushrooms

Buy a book on mushrooms and learn to identify them. Stress to your children the importance of not eating wild mushrooms because many can be toxic.

Take pictures of the mushrooms with a close-up lens.

See how many different kinds of mushrooms you can identify. Keep a list.

Attend a mycology exhibit.

Buy various kinds of mushrooms at your local market and learn to cook and eat them.

Visit a mushroom farm.

Wild Edible Plants

Buy a book and learn to identify various kinds of wild edible plants.

Make a whole meal of these plants.

Wildflowers

There are thousands upon thousands of wildflowers. Just when you think you've seen and identified every one in your area, you discover a new one.

Buy a wildflower identification book and see how many you can find and identify in a single summer.

Collect and press samples of all kinds of wildflowers in your area. Squeeze them in a flower press or in the pages of a book until they are dry. When they are dry, mount them on cards and cover with clear plastic wrap to preserve them.

Look tiny. Some exquisite wildflowers are half the size of your little fingernail. Lie down in a meadow and look tiny. See what is there.

Lie in a field of daisies and watch the clouds sail past.

Take home a bouquet of wildflowers (if picking is allowed and if there are plenty of the variety of flowers you are gathering).

Make a daisy chain and wear it or make a circlet for your hair.

Pretend you are a butterfly and flit from one flower to the next in complete abandon.

Bridges

You wouldn't think bridges could be an adventure category, but there are so many kinds of bridges that they can be very interesting.

See how many different kinds of bridges you can identify in your area.

There are cable-suspension bridges, drawbridges, bridges that turn to let boats through, floating bridges, high-rise bridges, swinging bridges, and logs over creeks. In some places, there are still covered bridges.

Visit the London Bridge in Arizona.

Walk across the Golden Gate Bridge in San Francisco.

Visit a Japanese garden and climb over the high curved bridges there.

Walk an abandoned railroad trestle for a real thrill.

Count how many bridges there are within a ten-mile radius of your house.

Find out if there are any covered bridges in your area. Visit them and take pictures. Find out who made them and why.

Canyons

There are all kinds of canyons to see. Some are just little narrow ones in the woods. Others, like the Grand Canyon, are too huge to comprehend.

Find out where the canyons are in your area.

What other attractions are near the canyon that might prove an adventure for your family?

Visit the massive Grand Canyon in Arizona. Take a burro ride to the bottom of it.

Visit Royal Gorge in Colorado.

Visit the canyon of the Yellowstone River in Yellowstone National Park.

Visit a canyon that has a swinging bridge hanging over it. Bounce your way back and forth across the bridge.

Caves

There are four kinds of caves: limestone, ice, talus, and lava tubes. The kind most of us are familiar with is the limestone cave with stalactites and stalagmites in wonderful formations. An ice cave is formed in areas where snow recedes and leaves a huge circular tunnel. The talus cave is formed by the laying down of debris at the base of a cliff or mountain. It is usually the result of glacial action. A lava tube cave is one where lava flowed out many thousands of years ago and left a hollow tube in the earth.

Find out what caves are in your area and tour them.

Watch for caves to visit when you are traveling. There are Mammoth Cave in Kentucky, Carlsbad Caverns in New Mexico, Sea Lions Caves in Oregon, and many more in between.

Join a spelunkers' club. Spelunkers are people who explore and study caves, usually uncharted ones.

Cemeteries

Believe it or not, cemeteries can be lots of fun.

Find an old cemetery and go there with large sheets of white paper and black charcoal, pastels, or color crayons. Lay the paper over the inscription on a tombstone and rub it with the crayon. It will bring up the pattern and lettering on the tombstone even though it may be almost unreadable otherwise.

Note the ages of those who have died. Notice that many died very young. Talk about the hardships they endured and how much better life is today.

Churches and Missions

Churches and missions are fun to collect with a camera. Perhaps you have a budding photographer in your family who can learn to take good pictures of these buildings.

Watch for churches in the towns, villages, and cities you visit. Every town has one or two beautiful churches.

In New England watch for the white-spired churches tucked in the mountains.

In the southwest watch for Spanish-style stucco and red-tiled-roof churches.

There are old missions all over this country. Watch for them and visit them. Many are now state parks.

Wander through the old churches and missions. Teach your children to respect these places of worship. Talk with them about the hardships early missionaries and pastors endured to bring the gospel to this country.

View the movie *The Mission* for a better understanding of what it cost to open certain mission fields.

Watch for organ concerts and special events at city churches throughout the land.

Take your children to services of faiths different than your own and help them respect other people's beliefs, traditions, and customs.

Cities

Cities are exciting places. Pick a city—any city—and decide to visit it. Before you go, order free materials from the chamber of commerce of that city so that you know what is available to see and do there. Let your children send for these materials.

Determine to learn about that city while you are visiting there and catch the flavor of the place.

Cities have many neighborhoods, each with its own flavor. Explore these in depth. Poke in and out of shops, restaurants, markets, factories, and places of worship.

See the city's art museums, special features, zoos, parks, bridges, and downtown shopping area.

Learn about the city's sports teams and attend a game if you can.

Clocks

Go to a clock shop and look at all the different kinds of time-pieces that are available.

Watch for clocks in towers of buildings.

Watch for street clocks. I've seen marvelous old steam clocks. It looks so strange to see steam coming from a clock.

Look for old clocks in museums and antique shops.

Buy an old clock at a thrift store. Let the kids take it apart.

Invest in a fine clock with chimes and pendulums.

Coins

Coin collecting can be a fun hobby for the entire family.

Visit a coin shop and have the owner show you his collection.

Buy some folders for pennies and let the kids start collecting.

Go to a coin show where many dealers get together and sell coins. Coin dealers are like a fraternity. They all know each other and they soon learn about their customers as well.

Get some books to help you identify coins.

Collecting coins from foreign countries can be lots of fun and very educational as well. The study of the coinage of a certain country may create a real interest in the culture, geography, and history of that country. Collecting foreign coins is not as good an investment as collecting U.S. coins, but in most cases they cost less to collect.

If one of your children becomes an avid coin collector, invest in some gold coins for her. Some can be obtained for less than fifty dollars.

Communications

Communication facilities like TV and radio stations can provide an evening of adventure for your family.

Visit the local TV stations. Some have programming that welcomes local guests. Try to get tickets and go to the show.

Visit a radio station and watch the disc jockeys at work. It can be an eye-opening experience for your kids to see the faces of their favorite radio voices.

Get tickets to watch the filming of weekly sitcoms or other favorite network programs when you are in the Los Angeles area. Tickets are free but must be obtained ahead of time.

Computers

It's definitely the age of the computer, and your kids probably know more about computers than you do. Perhaps you need to let them lead you on an adventure pursuing computers.

Visit a computer store and see what systems and games are available.

Visit a firm or factory that has a big computer operation.

Almost every home now has or soon will have a computer. Buy some new games to play together on the computer.

Spend an evening exploring the Internet. Discover new Web sites. Give strong guidance to your children about Internet usage to avoid their exposure to a predator.

Costumes

Kids love costumes, and there are all kinds of places to see them. Make an adventure out of costumes.

Go to a photo shop where they dress you up in old-fashioned costumes and have a family picture taken. It's lots of fun.

Visit a museum that has a costume display.

Go to a costume shop and buy costume making materials.

Go to a thrift shop and buy old clothes to make into costumes.

Attend an ethnic festival where everyone is dressed in costumes.

Cultures

Throughout this book I have talked about the interesting adventures a family can pursue related to studying the diverse cultural backgrounds of the American population. We are a divergent group of people, and discovering that can be a great adventure for your family.

Watch for seasonal ethnic events and go to them.

Take part in food fairs that are centered around ethnic foods.

Go to church services and celebrations that have an ethnic emphasis.

Make or buy various kinds of ethnic costumes.

Tour ethnic neighborhoods in your city.

D

Dams

Most dams also have a power plant nearby, and some also have fish ladders. These can be interesting to visit.

Tour a power plant.

Drive across the top of the dam, if there is a roadway and it is allowed.

Look for different kinds of dams—earth-filled, concrete, or even a beaver dam.

Look at the displays that show how the dam was built.

Find out how many dams are in your area. Try to visit them all.

Find out how the fish ladder works and watch for migrating fish.

Deserts

Deserts look very barren at first but they are fascinating places.

Read about life on the desert.

Rent and view a Walt Disney video that shows animal life on the desert.

Go to a desert and observe carefully.

Look for desert birds.

Look for desert animals.

Are there cactuses? What kind are they? When do the cactuses bloom? Be there to see it.

Take a burro ride in the desert.

Enjoy the solitude of the desert.

Drama

Attend drama productions at local high schools, colleges, and theaters.

Dramatize a play for your neighbors and friends.

Watch for drama productions in shopping malls, parks, and churches.

See if you can go backstage and meet some of the performers.

Work together as a family and write a play.

Eggs

Visit a poultry farm and see how eggs are produced, candled, and crated for shipment.

Visit a hatchery and see young chicks emerging from their shells.

Eat an omelet in a restaurant that specializes in them.

Watch for a Ukrainian craftsman who decorates eggs using a wax resist-and-dye method.

Factories

Factories are exciting places to visit. There are all kinds of factories to tour. Most factories have guided tours. Take advantage of this free adventure.

Go to a breakfast cereal factory.

See steel being made.

Visit a fabric mill.

Tour an automobile factory.

Tour an airplane factory.

Visit a food processing plant.

Visit a lumber mill.

Visit a meatpacking plant.

Tour a candy factory.

Look around your area and see what is available.

Fairs and Expositions

Every summer there are many fairs and expositions. Each is unique.

Make a day of going to the county or state fair.

Ride the rides, see the exhibits, and eat the foods.

Prepare an exhibit for a fair. Make it a family project.

Fall Color

In most areas of the country there are fall color displays. In fact one of the national news networks gives a daily update of fall color on the morning news show.

Take a drive through a high-color area.

Learn what makes the leaves change to different colors.

Gather bouquets of leaves to take home with you.

Take pictures.

Plan a vacation to New England in time to see the color.

Farming

There was a time when farming was a true adventure for a family to pursue—farming was their livelihood. Now there are fewer and fewer people making their living farming, and our kids know less and less about how food is produced.

Visit a dairy barn and watch the milking process. In most large dairies, it is a high-tech operation.

Get out somewhere and see the wheat and corn harvests.

Visit a horse ranch in the spring and see the new colts and fillies.

Visit a cattle ranch at branding time.

See if you can arrange a visit to a sheep ranch either at lambing time or at sheepshearing time.

Fashion

Attend a fashion show at a local department store.

Take a class in fashion.

Go to a local mall and see the changing fashions.

Learn how to make something to wear.

Get a book from the library and see how fashion has changed throughout history.

See what fashions have been retained over the years.

Talk and think about how fashion is influenced by well-known personalities and world events.

Feasts and Festivals

Keep checking your local newspaper for these events, and take your kids to them. There are winter carnivals, autumn leaf festivals, medieval festivals, pageants, and Native American festivals all waiting to be discovered.

Firefighting

Visit the local fire station. Ask for a tour.

If there is a smoke-jumper facility associated with the National Forest Service near you, visit it and find out what is happening there.

Go see a fire, but be sure to stay out of the way.

Encourage fire safety in your children.

Talk with them about the dangers of playing with matches.

Fish

Visit a large aquarium. There are many superb ones throughout the country.

Go fishing—fly-fishing, deep-sea fishing, trolling, lake fishing, ice-fishing, and fishing from a dock.

If you don't fish, go to a local fishing area and talk with the fishermen. They'll tell you all kinds of stories.

Go snorkeling, and view the fish in their own environment.

For the really adventurous, take a course in scuba diving.

Forests and Woods

There are all kinds of forests across the country. Most of them have both guided and unguided nature walks.

The forests are often on public lands and belong to all of us. We can use them free of charge.

Have a picnic in the woods.

Camp out in the woods.

Walk softly and watch for forest creatures.

Learn to know what plants and animals are in the woods. It will make the woods feel as comfortable to you as your own living room.

Forts

Old, usually reconstructed forts are interesting places to visit. They are scattered all over the country.

Visit a fort and talk about what it would have been like to live there with no running water, no sanitation facilities, no electricity, and with an enemy outside the gates.

Fossils

Fossils can be found everywhere. They are inside rocks, in clay banks, in gravel bars, and at the seashore.

Find out if there is a fossil deposit in your area, and see if it is all right to gather fossil samples.

Go to a museum and look at the fossil samples.

Visit Dinosaurland near Vernal, Utah, and see the unearthing of a bank full of dinosaur bones. Some scientists have worked on the same fossil for thirty years.

Furniture

Visit a furniture factory.

Visit an upholstery shop and watch furniture being restored.

Hunt for antique furniture.

Learn about different styles of furniture.

Geology

Your family can have many adventures learning about geology and rockhounding.

Visit a geological display in a museum.

Visit a mining museum.

Find out where the local rock hounds go and what they are looking for. Ask if your family can go along.

Learn to identify the different kinds of rocks. If your kids have studied science in school, they may be able to help you.

Ghost Towns

The West has numerous abandoned ghost towns that are fun to visit.

Try to figure out what each building's original purpose was.

Pick up bits of broken pottery and study the design.

Pretend you lived there in the town's heyday.

Glaciers

If you live where there are glaciers, visit one and study what happens when a glacier moves through an area.

Look for the U-shaped valleys that indicate a glacier has gone that way in times past.

If you are visiting a glacier, look for the glacial milk that flows from beneath it. This is powder-fine silt suspended in water. It gives the rivers a milky look.

Glassblowing

Craft shows, fairs, and specialty malls often have glassblowers at work. Watch them.

Colonial craft exhibits sometimes have glassblowers at work.

Government

Visit government buildings.
Go to see your state legislature in action.
Go to see the United States Congress in action.
Talk about government.

Hobby Shows

In most cities there are hobby shows once or twice a year. Go to them.

Also in many cities there are model-train clubs.

Find out if there is go-cart racing in your town.

Hot-Air Balloons

Go to the area where hot-air balloons are being flown and watch these beautiful creations lift off from the ground.

Pay for your kids to ride in a hot-air balloon.

Talk about the scientific principles that make a hot-air balloon fly.

Insects

Collect insects and identify them.

Get a book and learn all about insects.

Many children are afraid of insects but if they learn which are harmful and which are helpful, they will lose some of their fear.

Juggling

Learn how to juggle. Do it together as a family.
Go see a clown who knows how to juggle.
Watch for street jugglers.

Kite Flying

Buy a good kite and fly it together as a family. Kite flying never loses its appeal.

Go to a kite store and see all the beautiful kites that are available.
Read about the history of kite flying.
Try building a kite together.
Watch for kite-flying exhibitions.

Lakes

Lakes offer all kinds of family fun.
Sail a boat.
Swim.
Fish.
Loaf on the shore.
Hike to high mountain lakes where only the hardy go.

Law enforcement

Visit law enforcement agencies. See what the police department in your city does in the way of public relations.

Visit the FBI in Washington, D.C.
Visit a courtroom and observe the process of law at work.

Lighthouses

Collect lighthouses with a camera. See how many different kinds you can discover.

Read about the history of individual lighthouses.

Tour a lighthouse if possible.

Medicine

Visit an interesting nearby medical facility. Take a tour if one is available. Seeing such a facility and learning what happens there may help your children be less afraid if they have to go to a hospital one day.

Meteorology

Visit a weather station and learn what happens there.
Keep charts and graphs of your weather.
Learn about clouds and what weather changes they signify.
Learn the dangers of lightning and thunderstorms.
Learn how hail is formed.
Look for exhibits in science museums that tell about weather.

Military

Visit a military installation.
Watch a military parade.
Learn about the different branches of the service and the uniforms they wear.

Mining

Learn about different mining operations.
Find out about touring a mine.
Some museums now have simulated mine shafts to give you a feel for the miner's lot in life.

Mountains

Take a trip to the mountains.

Go skiing.

Go camping.

Hike in the mountains.

Go to the top of the mountains on a clear day and see if you can see forever.

Music

Go to the symphony.

Go to the opera.

Go hear old-time fiddling.

Find a good banjo player and watch his fingers fly.

Listen to all kinds of music and learn to appreciate them all.

Listen to music and draw pictures about what you think the music is saying.

Write new words to an old tune.

Nature Trails

Nature trails are a good learning adventure and also a great place to run off steam.

Watch for something you've never seen before—perhaps a flower or a mushroom. You'll probably find it.

Neighborhoods

Walk through your city's neighborhoods and discover what is unique about them.

Browse through all the little shops.

Talk to the people who live there. How long have they been there? Why have they never moved from there? What is the best feature about their neighborhood?

Oceanography

Visit the ocean beaches and walk along them while beach-combing.

Swim or wade in the ocean.

Find out where you can watch whales migrating. Some places even offer boat rides to watch the whales.

Learn about the shore birds that nest along the coasts.

Learn about life in the tide pools.

Origami

Ask someone who knows this Japanese craft of folding paper into decorative shapes to teach your family how to do some simple pieces.

Parks

There are all kinds of parks in every city and town. Most of them have some distinctive characteristic. Find out what that is.

Visit our national parks. They are a great heritage and a great treasure. Take advantage of them.

Pottery

Pottery works are spread around the country. Some are small shops owned by individuals and some are huge factories that make dishes by the thousands.

See what's available in your area and take a tour.

Get some clay and make your own pottery.

Take a pottery class as a family.

Quilts

Hand-pieced quilts are coming back in fashion. They are sold at top dollar as true works of art.

Visit a quilt show and see some modern craftsmanship.

Visit a museum where old quilts are displayed. Remember that these were made without the aid of sewing machines and modern conveniences. All work was done by hand.

Rodeos

Rodeos are wild, fun events. Take your kids and enjoy the performance of cowboys and animals.

Talk to a cowboy or cowgirl.

Skiing

More and more families are learning to cross-country or downhill ski. Cross-country skiing probably provides more time for family togetherness than downhill, but most young people prefer the speed of downhill skiing.

Once you learn to ski, there are all kinds of places to go skiing.

Snowmobiling

Snowmobiling is an increasingly popular sport. Many families belong to snowmobiling clubs and get out regularly in the wintertime.

Sports Events

There is no limit to the sports events your family can attend at any season of the year. Professional sports are expensive, but there are many local sporting programs that are virtually free.

Learn a sport and play it together.

Theme Parks

There are a number of great theme parks around the nation, such as Disneyland, Walt Disney World, Seaworld, and Six Flags Over Texas. They are great fun for families.

Toys

Toy stores are fun for the whole family to visit. Even if you don't buy a lot of toys, it is still fun to look and maybe even try out the display models.

Transportation

Learn about all methods of transportation. Remember that as your children become familiar with all modes of transportation, they will be unafraid later in life to travel on their own and continue to have their own adventures.

Take a boat ride.

Take a train ride even if it is just to the next city.

Visit a switching yard for trains.

Ride in a double-decker bus if possible.

Take a bus trip.

Universities and Colleges

If you hope that your children will attend college, then it is a good idea to introduce them to some of the campuses in your area.

Attend a play on the college campus.
Attend a musical event.
Visit the campus museum.
Go to the college library.
Have lunch in the student union building.
Look at some of the colleges' catalogs, especially if your children are teenagers.

Vegetables

Visit a farmers' market and try some new fruits and vegetables you've never eaten. Let the kids make the selections.

Talk to the farmers. Learn where they grow their vegetables, why they grow them, how long they've been vegetable gardeners, and anything else you can get them to tell you.

Grow a vegetable garden.

Wood Carving

There are still some fine craftsmen who do wood carving. Find them and watch them at work.

There are shows that display driftwood, which has been polished to a furniture-like finish.

Xylophones and Other Musical Instruments

Go to a musical instrument store and talk to the owner about the various kinds of instruments he sells.

Visit someone who makes musical instruments.

Invite someone who plays a musical instrument to your home and have him share his music and something about the instrument (the more exotic the better).

Have the children make their own musical instruments from combs and paper, pot lids, empty cardboard boxes, and other household items.

Make your own xylophone by filling glasses with water to various levels.

Yacht Racing

If you are in an area of the country where they are held, attend a yacht race.

Watch the America's Cup yacht races on television.

Try to find someone with a yacht and have him take you for a sail.

Zoos

Who doesn't love a zoo? Kids do, that's for sure. You can go again and again, and each time see something you have never seen before.

Help your children learn to be observant and quiet when watching the animals.

Part **2**

Finding Time for Family Fun

There are enough time-consuming tasks in the everyday life of a family to threaten *every* family member with having "no time to be me."

God did not intend the home to be a place of confusion and task-driven people. Our homes don't need to be that way. What we all must do is evaluate our lifestyle, our use of time, and our attitude toward time.

Is time a short-shrift gift from God, or could it be that he gave us exactly the amount of time we need to accomplish what he needs done? Intellectually we all know the right answer to that question. He gave us exactly the amount of time we need. But how do we make it work in our individual life and in family life? Let's see.

What does the number 168 mean to you? It is a number that is important to everyone. It is the number of hours in a week. Every living person gets the same number of hours each week, yet some people get so much more accomplished with their portion of time than others do. Why?

Let's take a look at some of the ways we use a week's worth of time:

Sleep	8 hours x 7 days a week	= 56 hours
Grooming	2 hours x 7 days a week (Before you say, "I don't spend that much time grooming," think of time spent getting haircuts, perms, doing your nails, etc.)	= 14 hours
Work, school	8 hours x 5 days a week	= 40 hours
Commuting	7 hours (plus or minus)	7 hours
Eating and food-related activity	3 hours a day x 7 days a week	= 21 hours
Total		138 hours

One hundred thirty-eight hours. That still leaves you thirty hours to do as you wish. But suppose that what you wish is to spend three hours every evening watching television. Now you have only nine hours left. Still, a lot can be accomplished in nine hours, if the time is used wisely.

Ephesians 5:15–17 in the Phillips translation of the New Testament says:

> Live life, then, with a due sense of responsibility, not as men who do not know the meaning and purpose of life but as *those who do*. Make the best use of your time, despite all the difficulties of these days. Don't be vague, but firmly grasp what you know to be the will of God.

At some point we must decide what needs to be done and what can go undone. We feel guilty when our expectations for ourselves, our kids, and our families are too high. We want everything to be perfect all the time. That is unrealistic but it is encouraged by what we see on television and read in women's magazines.

There is also the myth of togetherness that makes us feel guilty. This myth says that we must spend a great deal of time together to get to know one another. It helps a family to have a lot of time together, but it is just as important to learn to buy up opportunities and use available time wisely, whether working or playing. Maybe "less done better" is a slogan we should adopt and a goal we should strive for.

This section of the book is all about finding solutions to time problems. But here, let's summarize what we can do about the guilt problem. Here are some suggestions:

Be realistic about your situation. You're single and have to work hard to keep bread on the table. You don't have a lot of extra time or strength to spend with your kids. That's the way it is. Accept it and then begin to look for solutions.

You're a traveling dad and you're gone more than you are home. Analyze why you've chosen this profession. Is it right for you? Is this the way it's going to be? If the answers are yes, then start looking for the best in the situation.

You're a busy full-time mother, yet you still wrestle with guilt. Why? What is the source of your guilt? Is it self-imposed or is it placed on you by someone outside your situation and family? Is it any of that person's business? Settle it once and for all in your mind.

You're an eight-to-five dad whose livelihood depends on extracurricular homework and/or involvement in work-related and civic activities. What can you do about it? Is this the way it's going to be? If yes, then settle it in your mind and get on with life.

Perhaps nothing is as debilitating to excellence in family life as parents who make decisions on the basis of guilt. Letting kids stay up late and rule the roost just because we feel guilty about the amount of time we spend with them is an invitation to disaster.

Determine to make the best of it. And who knows what that may be. The best for your family is limited only by your imagination. How can you make this family life work smoothly so that every person feels cherished and not neglected?

Learn to use bits of time. I love to get down to the level of a small child's eyes and just look at him and

Learn to use bits of time.

smile. Almost every child responds positively to that treatment. I sometimes wonder if any grown-up, way-up-there, tall person has bent down to talk to this little person all day.

Do the same with your little ones. It doesn't take a lot of time to clear your mind of whatever fills it and concentrate intently on your child. Look in his eyes and listen with both your ears and your heart. Give yourself to this moment in time.

Use time wisely. That's what the rest of this part of the book is about. It is full of ideas taken from the business world, from consultants in the time management field, and from the true experts, parents who have found ways to have time for kids, no matter what their schedule.

Make some decisions about what you can and cannot do and then live with those decisions. You have twenty-four hours each day—no more and no less. You have to acknowledge the law of supply and demand. And you have to cut the demands down to the supply.

Try to have a master schedule with every family member's activities posted. This may not be something you want to do on a continuing basis, but until you get a handle on why everyone in your family always feels so rushed, it may be helpful. You will probably be astonished at the number of activities your family is doing. Begin to deal with cutting down the activities on your master schedule to an amount that can be handled.

Realize you are not supermom and superdad. You are just ordinary people with ordinary reserves of strength. Use that strength wisely and save some of it for the most important people in your lives: your children and each other.

Do not let others lay their guilt trips on you. It doesn't matter what the magazines say you should do. It doesn't matter what television commentators or civic or

Gain the most time possible for family life and use that time wisely.

church leaders say. Each family and each person must find the level of activity that works well.

Perhaps some of the greatest guilt inducers are grandparents and other family members: "You should . . ." or "You shouldn't . . ." or "We never did it that way. We always . . ." Because we are so used to listening to and obeying our parents, we think about what they've said and it begins to produce guilt.

The truth is that this is your life, your house, your kids. You have to find a way to manage your time and develop a lifestyle that fits your family.

Learn to say no. Saying no to opportunities to sit on committees, sponsor clubs, and get involved in worthwhile service organizations can be painful at first. There are so many good things that need to be done and so few willing volunteers, but if we are going to be able to give quality time to our priorities, we must learn to say no to some activities. Over and above not having time for our priorities, we can spread ourselves so thin that nothing is done well.

If no one but you is laying on the guilt, because you are comparing your family with someone else's, stop it. Most other people have problems of their own and are, just like you, trying to cope day-to-day. They are not even going to notice your family's situation.

Your most important goal is to gain the most time possible for family life and to use that time wisely. God gave us enough time for what he wants us to do. We must find out what he wants and then do it.

Remember that life changes as we go along. There may well be time later for those things we cannot do now.

9

Looking for Time

Accomplishing Major Projects

A Plan of Action

If what needs to be done is deemed important, the next question is, how important? Is it important enough to give it five minutes a day? If the answer is yes, then you must plan a way to get five minutes a day for that important thing.

I don't know how many times I have heard about authors who have written complete books, one page at a time. By setting a goal of writing one page a day—only one page—they have finished many books. Think about it. One page each day equals 365 pages a year. That's a sizable book. How many people talk about writing a book someday and never get a single word on paper in a whole year?

The biggest problem with handling our time well is that we don't know what is important and what is not. Here's a way to help you determine that.

Step 1. Get a piece of paper and write down all the things you *want* to do, all the things you *must* do, and all the things you *should* do. Don't forget to include chauffeuring kids to doctors, ball games, lessons, and so on. Think about social and civic obligations. Also remember school functions (if the kids remember to tell you about them).

Step 2. Now look at your list and ask yourself which of these items are the most important. Write *As* beside them. There may be several *As*, but not everything on your list can be top priority.

Step 3. Now ask yourself which are next most important items and put *Bs* beside them.

Step 4. Beside all the remaining, write *Cs*.

Step 5. If you can, eliminate all the *Cs*. "What?" you say. "But there are some things listed that I must do." All right, then, move them to a different priority. If there are some things there that you would like to do, ask yourself if, realistically, you will ever get to them. Are they going to be a constant source of frustration to you? Perhaps you can get a box, a file drawer, or a cupboard, dump all the *C* priorities into it, and deal with them someday—maybe. Or maybe a day will come when you will open the storage area and dump the entire contents into the trash, where you probably should have put it in the first place.

Try "Swiss cheesing," poking holes in big projects.

Step 6. Now look at the *As*. Which is the most important item of all? Label it *A-1*. Next in importance? *A-2*. And so on through the list. This is not a very original idea. It is used in most time management seminars and efficiency studies. It was developed by Alan Lakein many years ago, and it is still around because it works.

Put your *A* priority list someplace you can see it all the time and then begin working away at it, doing *A-1* first, *A-2* second, and so on. Give yourself the satisfaction of drawing a big black line through completed tasks.

But perhaps your *A-1* is a huge project such as painting the house, landscaping the yard, or learning French, and it will take you a long time to do it. Just remember, if it truly is *A-1* in importance, you must find at least five minutes a day to work on it. This can be accomplished by an idea called "Swiss cheesing," or poking small holes in a large project—whittling away at it until it is finished.

Step 7. When you have finished your *A* list, turn to your *B* list and keep working at it until it too is finished. Then it is time for a new session of listing and prioritizing activities.

Some people make daily lists and some make weekly ones. Others make long-term lists. Do whatever works best for you. Let's consider that on your list is a very important, long-term goal. How do you go about accomplishing it?

One way is to write that item by itself on a piece of paper. Beneath it, list all the necessary things you must do to accomplish that goal. Let's take learning French for an example.

How can you reach this goal? Your plan might look something like this.

1. Find out what community college teaches a beginners French class at night.
2. Find out on what nights the class is held.
3. Find out how much it costs.
4. Determine who will care for your children while you take the class.
5. Determine how much homework will be required.
6. Decide if this is the best time to take the class when all the above is considered.
7. Enroll in the class.
8. Purchase the books.
9. Go to the first class.

Now you have a plan of action to accomplish your goal. All you have to do is go for it! Put the first item, "Find out what college," on your daily "to do" list. Put the second one on the next day's "to do" list. By the end of the week, you will have completed seven steps toward your long-term, *A-1* priority.

A priorities are worth every bit of time we put into them, but *C* priorities rarely are. Alan Lakein said, "It's not worthwhile to make a big effort for a task of little value. On the other hand a project of high value can be worth a great deal of effort."[1]

The importance of Planning

Planning gives direction to our lives. Not planning is a kind of plan in itself—a plan to let time control us rather than our controlling time. Only ten minutes a day spent thinking about priorities, and a few minutes once a week to see what kind of progress we are making, is all that is needed.

Planning eliminates the "if only" syndrome, *If only* I had learned French. *If only* I had taken the time to visit my friend when she was sick. *If only* I had played more with the kids when they were little. *If only* I had taken the time to talk with them about sex and drugs.

Planning brings the future into the present so you can do something about it. Planning helps to eliminate the chronic tiredness that comes from spending more time thinking about the work than doing it. Planning helps you decide whether or not you are trying to do more than you should be doing.

The secret of successful time management lies not in seeing how much you can cram into a tight time frame, not in clock-watching, but in getting control of your time by carefully planning what you are going to do each day.

The time you allot to each task is determined by your priorities. If you have an hour to spare, ask yourself, *What is the best use of my time now?* Then think about your *A-1* priority. Is this the time to work on that *A-1* priority—to make some headway toward learning French, for example? Could you study for an hour? Could you memorize a list of words in that hour? What could you do toward reaching your goal in that hour?

Some people are freshest in the morning and use that time to lay their plan for the day. Some like evening planning better, when they can evaluate the present day's activities and see what progress they have made, then lay plans for the next day.

There is no right or wrong time to plan. It is a matter of determining what works best for you. If you neglect to plan, you may still accomplish much, but your accomplishments may be scattered and not in the direction of the important priorities in your life.

Hoẅ to Plań

I had a friend who was working on her master's degree in English. One day when we were having lunch together, she said to me, "I'm having an awful time getting to my thesis. Every time

I settle down to work on it, the phone rings and it is someone who needs counsel or prayer, or one of my kids needing help, or a friend wants to go shopping or have lunch." I had to chuckle at that, as I, her friend, sat eating my salad with her.

But her problem was genuine. I suggested to her, "Why don't you take your calendar and mark off a hunk of time each week. Make it right in the middle of your prime operating time, the time when you feel best and are most productive. Then respect that as an appointment that cannot be broken. When some-one calls, just say, 'I'm sorry. I can't go to lunch. I have an appointment.'"

I don't know if she did what I suggested but I know that very soon her thesis was written and she had her master's degree.

Blocking out time on your calendar to work on a major proj-ect is a good plan and perhaps the only one for making head-way on a project that is a top priority in your life.

Take your calendar and your prime goals and block out large sections of time to work on your projects. For families, espe-cially those with young children at home, there is no finer goal or priority than to give time to your children. What will you do with the blocked-out time? Does a child need help with school-work? Is she struggling with multiplication tables? Does she really understand what she is reading? Does she need you to lis-ten to her musical achievements and encourage her? Does she need you to just listen while she tells you her fears and joys? Does she need time for roughhousing on the living room floor? Does the family need to get together and do some planning or clearing the air?

In your planning, remember that relaxation is a good use of time. Mothers, don't forget to schedule some quiet or fun times for yourself. Too often mothers plan for everyone else and for-get that unless they have time to regroup, they don't have much to offer their family.

In a book called *Leave Yourself Alone,* Eugenia Price said, "When possible, I legislate into every day at least an hour in the silence—walking alone, just holding a book, still unopened—a truly quiet time without the sound of anything to drain or diminish the part of me which must be strong if I am to leave myself alone and focus on God."[2]

Pat King, another writer, says, "Since God is a generous God, it makes sense that He has given us time in abundance for everything He has called us to do."[3]

Planning helps me to not carry so much stuff in my head. For example, if I know I will be speaking in six weeks and I lay a plan for working toward that event, I don't have to worry or even think about what needs to be done until it comes up on my calendar. I take time to plan when I will do each task so that I am ready for the workshop in six weeks. Then I enter it all into my daily calendar. I don't think about a task until it comes up on the calendar, then I deal with it. If I cannot settle an item on the day I should, I move it to the next day and the next until it is accomplished.

It is very freeing not to carry around a lot of mental baggage and guilt about what I should be doing. Planning frees my mind to work on the projects at hand.

What You Can Do

The amazing thing is that when we have a plan, a "to do" list, we often find pockets of extra time between major tasks. It is amazing what can be accomplished in those pockets of time. For example, with five minutes you can:

call a friend and schedule lunch
comb your hair, brush your teeth, and freshen up
write a thank-you note
water a plant
place a catalog order
clean a mirror
make a bed
microwave a bag of popcorn

With ten minutes you can:

pick out a card for a friend at a store
fix a snack for a child
repot a plant

put a load of clothes in the washer
call for tickets to a play or other event
read a few pages in a book or magazine
dust some furniture
polish your shoes

With thirty minutes you can:

read a couple of chapters in a book
shop for groceries
check your bank statement
pay some bills
work on a craft project
clean your workshop
prepare a casserole for dinner
go to the library and check out some books
take a leisurely bath
mow the grass or weed a flower bed

It probably isn't necessary to put your daily routine on a "to do" list. You know you have to shower, brush your teeth, and so on. Write down the nonroutine things you must do and would like to do before bedtime.

Keep the plan as loose as possible. No one enjoys being tied to a rigid schedule. If something comes up that is more important than what is on your list, do it and forget the "to do" list.

Nothing is more debilitating than setting goals that are too high to reach. Make your goals realistic. Give yourself the opportunity to learn how to manage time. It takes a while to get comfortable with a time management idea and plan. So stretch but not so far that your attempt at time management topples over.

Help! It's Gaining on Me!

Organizing Household Chores

Good organization in a household gives a sense of stability and peace to the family. It helps family members learn how to organize themselves and it provides pockets of time for family fun, free from the "I should be doing something else" syndrome.

Organization of household chores takes time and thought—lots of it—in the beginning. But once the systems and plans are in place and once they become automatic, you'll be glad you took the time to get organized.

Plan Ahead

Just as with major projects you want to accomplish, you must prioritize household chores to be sure the most important things actually are done. So, do the most important things first. Then proceed to the next most important tasks, then to the third most important, and if you ever get to them, do the least important tasks last. That means you have to know what needs to be done first, second, third, and so on. You have to think and plan.

A good plan for keeping your household in order is to do the dailies first. Picking up has to be done either by you, or if they are old enough, children who may have dropped the items. Beds need to be made daily, dishes done, and maybe floors swept.

A simple rule I try to follow is: Never leave a room in the morning until everything is in order. It isn't as impossible as it sounds. A quick look around the bathroom before you leave it in the morning will reveal towels that didn't quite get hung up, clothes that almost made it into the hamper, and a tube of toothpaste without a cap. In a couple of minutes you can swoop those socks into the hamper and the toothpaste into a drawer. Then grab those towels and use one of them to give the countertop and fixtures a quick polish. Hang up some fresh towels, then pause at the door and look back. What you'll see is a neat room. Take the damp towels and drop them in the washer on your way through the house. Continue through all the other rooms in the same way.

Next, plan a large chunk of time when you can do some serious cleaning. Plan to do more than the dailies but less than a major housecleaning. This can be a weekend blitz or a couple of hours two or three times a week. Do the laundry, vacuum the rugs, dust, and whatever else is needed.

Try to stay on whatever kind of schedule you have established for yourself. This will keep you from getting behind and then having to expend more energy to catch up.

Don't start something you can't finish in the amount of time you have allotted yourself. Your daily cleaning time is not enough time to start a large project. Cleaning the garage or reorganizing the attic will have to wait until you can set aside a day for it. In all of your tasks, build in a cushion of time. Something or someone will almost always come along to slow you down or interrupt you.

Keeping Track of Tasks

I heard about a system established by two women who call themselves the Sidetracked Home Executives. I have never met either woman, although I've seen them interviewed on television numerous times. After watching their interviews, I established my own card system for keeping track of necessary duties at my house.

I determined what had to be done on a daily basis to maintain the standard of living I had set for my family. I wrote these tasks on a blue 3″ x 5″ card. The card looked something like this:

Dailies

Make beds.

Pick up clothes, toys, newspapers, etc.

Wash dishes (or put them in the dishwasher).

Sweep floors if necessary.

Start a load of laundry.

Doing the dailies usually takes about an hour each morning. Whether I am at home all day or working outside my home, I still follow the same morning routine.

On seven white 3″ x 5″ cards I recorded weekly tasks, the jobs that have to be done once a week, fifty-two times a year, such as laundry, ironing, vacuuming, cleaning the refrigerator, and so on.

The cards looked like this:

Monday:
Dust furniture in the living-room
and one bedroom. Vacuum rugs in
these same rooms.

Tuesday:
Clean refrigerator and make
shopping list at the same time.
Plan menus.

Then I took thirty pink cards and on each one wrote one task that needed to be done once a month. These were things like:

Day 1 *Wipe fingerprints from around light switches.*	*Day 3* *Dust lamp shades and light bulbs.*
Day 2 *Clean one kitchen drawer.*	*Day 4* *Sweep down cobwebs.*

I found that when I followed this plan faithfully, everything was taken care of in turn and I never had to think about it. If I didn't get something done one day and I felt it had to be done that month, I'd fasten the card to the refrigerator and do the job the next day or later in the week. It worked well.

I had twelve green cards, one for each month of the year. On these were bits of information and reminders of things that happened in those months that I needed to take care of. For example, the January card said, "Inventory towels and sheets. Shop white sales for needed items."

The November card had a note that said, "Make sure you have an outfit for the holidays," and another that said "Address Christmas card envelopes by end of month."

Here are some other ideas that might give you a start on your own file:

January

   Put away Christmas ornaments.

   Discard old ornaments and buy new ones on sale.

   Inventory sheets, towels, blankets and purchase needed
      items at this month's white sales.

February

Buy summer bulbs and seeds.

Plan family Valentine celebration.

March

Start yard cleanup.

Change smoke detector batteries.

April

Fertilize lawn.

Get flower beds ready and buy bedding plants.

Put away winter clothes.

Have winter coats cleaned or washed.

May

Choose and send Mother's Day card.

Plant garden.

Clean condenser coils on refrigerator and freezer (a once-a-year job).

June

Have mower serviced.

Have carpets cleaned.

July

Buy school clothes on sale.

August

Put fall fertilizer on lawns.

Check smoke detector batteries.

September

Put away summer clothes.

Check needs for winter coats, boots, gloves, caps, scarves, ski wear.

Replace furnace filter.

Have chimney cleaned.

October
> Have car winterized.
> Plan a pumpkin party.
> Put on storm windows.

November
> Plan Thanksgiving dinner.
> Do Christmas letter and cards.
> Make sure everyone has something nice to wear during
> the holidays.

December
> Purchase Christmas tree.
> Plan holiday entertaining.
> Do seasonal baking.

Ideas for once-a-year family events (birthdays, anniversaries, and so on) can also be put on these cards. You can write once-a-year family fun ideas on them: "The circus comes to town."

Making Lists

I recently asked a very young and very busy lady how she keeps track of tasks and appointments. "Lists," she replied. "I keep lists!" I have other friends who virtually live by lists. In fact most people I know who are well organized keep lists of some kind. Following are some ideas for keeping lists.

First, you need a place to keep your lists so you know where they are. A small loose-leaf notebook will work well. These are available at variety and stationery stores and are well worth the investment. If you use a daily planner or datebook, there is usually a place for keeping lists.

To be of the most value, this notebook should travel with you at all times for quick reference. If it is a loose-leaf notebook, tabs between sections will make it even more useful. If your notebook does not have tabs, you can buy them and attach at appropriate places.

What lists should your notebook have in it? That's up to you, but here are some ideas that have helped me and others:

Names, addresses, and telephone numbers

Birthday and anniversary information

Sizes of all family members

Colors you and other family members wear

Colors used in your home—paint chips and fabric swatches are helpful

Yard and home care—product names

Car care—servicing dates, products used, auto license expiration date, driver's license expiration date

Medical records—date and type of vaccination; phone numbers of doctors, dentists, and veterinarians

Location of important documents

Favorite restaurants and hotels—telephone numbers

Packing lists for traveling

Shopping lists

It will take considerable time to get your lists together, but you probably already have some of them, in rough form at least. You will need to expand your lists slowly and thoughtfully. You may not want or need all of these lists, but remember that every time you go searching for an address, phone number, size, or location of something, you are losing valuable time that could be better spent in family activity or even in doing absolutely nothing.

Speeding Up Shopping

For some people, shopping is recreation and it can be lots of fun when you have the time to do it. But for busy moms, especially if they work, shopping can be a real trial.

Perhaps one way to handle shopping is to get someone else to do it. I see lots of husbands in the grocery stores these days. Some men truly enjoy shopping and would gladly take on the task if asked.

Teenagers and young people who still live at home can be a great help when it comes to grocery shopping. It's good practice for them to learn to stay within a budget. If you want them to shop the way you shop and buy the way you buy, then you have to take them shopping and teach them well before the teen years.

In recent years, there has been a proliferation of catalog houses across the country. These houses usually have toll-free numbers and twenty-four-hour-a-day shopping, seven days a week. The quality of merchandise carried by these catalogs is often as good as that found in large department stores.

Once you get on a catalog list, other catalogs will find their way to your home. You'll have plenty of shopping opportunities. However, if you think that might not happen fast enough and you want to get on some catalog lists, check the backs of magazines where the small black and white, one-sixth-page ads are found. Most of those are for catalogs. Some are free and for some you pay a small fee that can be applied to a purchase.

Now you figure it out. Which is more time and cost efficient: a trip to a shopping mall—or maybe several trips if you are not sure which store has what you need—or sitting down for a few minutes with a phone and a catalog?

If you need to return merchandise, some catalog houses even pick up goods for free. Some will have the shipping company repackage the items for return shipping. You can't beat this system for saving money and time.

A good alternative to catalog shopping is to locate a store that carries almost everything a family could need and concentrate your buying there. Shopping at a store like this means you can buy for all your needs in one trip. You may also be able to take care of banking, getting film processed, and having prescriptions filled, along with other services, all in the same store.

Another way to make shopping easier is to make friends with owners of small shops. Get to know them and let them know you. The better you know each other, the more you can help each other.

Let them know your size, color, and fabric preference. Have them call you when special items they think you might like come in and when sales are about to happen. Become a preferred customer, one the proprietor thinks of first when a new shipment of merchandise arrives.

Some major department stores notify preferred customers of upcoming sales. Some even have special presale shopping hours for preferred customers.

Simplifying Your Lifestyle

Most of us have too many things in our home, office, and car. We end up moving these things from one spot to another and then moving them back again. Or we pick them up, clean under them, and put them down again.

Do you honestly have time to work around large collections of stuff? Would it be better if you reduced the amount of things you have to take care of and spent that time having fun with your kids?

Here are some ideas for simplifying your lifestyle.

Eliminate clutter. When I open a cupboard door and everything slides out on the floor, I know the time has come to deal with that mess. If possible, I like to deal with it right then. After all, it is all out on the floor anyway. Usually much of the clutter is things no one is using anymore or never used in the first place. Get a bag or box and realistically look at each object, asking yourself, *Who uses this? Do we need it? Could we live without it?* If the answer to the last question is yes, then drop it in the discard bag.

It's a good idea to remove the discard bag from the house before people begin poking through it and returning the contents to the shelf or other places in the house.

I suggest you go through one cupboard or closet each week and get rid of everything you have not used this year. You will be amazed how much easier it is to keep that area clean.

Pare down your wardrobe. Be honest with yourself. Are you hanging on to that dress or suit because you made a mistake when you bought it and you feel guilty? Find someone who could use it and give it away. Once it's gone you'll feel better, and so will the recipient.

Consider your plants. Plants take a lot of time. Do you really need them? The answer may be yes, and if it is, fine. I have a number of plants in my home. But believe me, they are easy-care plants. They thrive on neglect. If I find a plant taking too much time, or if it refuses to do what it is supposed to do—like bloom—out it goes.

Cut down the toy supply. Almost every child in America has three times as many toys as he needs. Children have so many toys that imagination has almost disappeared.

Help your child go through his toys at least once a year. Encourage him to discard broken or worn-out items, but don't demand that he part with a favorite toy. If that toy still has meaning to the child, let him keep it.

Talk with your children about giving away some of the toys they no longer play with. Most cities have a drive for used toys just before the holidays. Firehouse crews and other public servants repair and refurbish toys for needy tots. Help your children see that their cast-off items will bring great joy to others. This is a great opportunity to teach them about sharing.

It is also important to help your children cut down at the other end, where all this clutter begins. Help them to be satisfied with less. Every commercial they see on television encourages consumer greed. Yet, as so many of us have learned, the acquisition of those desired objects does not necessarily bring contentment and satisfaction. Help your children decide what they really want and not be pressured by commercialism.

Surviving the Paper Blizzard

How can you organize the paper blizzard that comes in the door almost every day? What should you do with the junk mail and the kids' precious papers?

One of the best ways to get control of paper clutter is to toss about 98 percent of it. Be ruthless in your tossing. Look at those magazines. Will you ever really go back and read them again? And is there anything as stale as a day-old newspaper? Add it to the recycle pile in the garage. Put the kids' school papers in a pile for them to sort through. Getting rid of stuff is a lifelong pursuit, and children might as well begin early learning how to sort and toss.

If papers are left unorganized, they can quickly overwhelm you and your home. But when you have a designated place for every important piece of paper, and you put it there, you save time and frustration and it is easier to keep your home neat.

Have a place to put bills. In our house it is an 8-1/2″ x 11″ stationery box without a lid. We keep it on a shelf in the office and drop the bills, credit card slips, and order forms or check stubs into it to be dealt with on bill-paying day.

On bill-paying day, the checks are written and then the paid bills and credit card slips are filed in a six-pocketed file and labeled by month. If we must return something to a store and need the sales slip, or a company says we haven't paid a bill and we have, it's easy to go back to the correct monthly pocket and find the canceled check, paid invoice, or sales slip.

Use file folders and a filing cabinet or get a small, metal, fireproof box or safe to store important papers such as birth or adoption certificates, marriage licenses, wills, insurance policies, records of stocks and bonds, military discharge papers, automobile titles, and real estate papers, including deeds, title insurance, closing statements, title abstract, and a copy of your mortgage. Either use the box or designate another place for warranty papers and instruction books.

You may want to consider getting a safe-deposit box as a place to store the above documents, and keep copies of them in your home.

Into your strongbox or safe you should also put a complete listing for each family member. It should have name, birth date, place of birth—including city, county, state, and nation—social security number, passport information, dates of inoculations, allergic reactions, and so on. Put in a record for your pet too.

There should also be information about who is designated as guardian of your children in the event of the death of both parents at the same time. Include the names and maiden names of both sets of grandparents, and if you are a woman, your maiden name, as these are often used as security identification for banks and high-security institutions. There should be names, addresses, and phone numbers of close relatives who could be reached quickly in the event of a tragedy.

Open the mail beside the garbage can.

The Internal Revenue Service recommends that you save tax records for three years. Anyone who has ever gone through an IRS audit is glad he saved old records. Put these in boxes and store them out of the way.

It will take some concentrated time and effort to get your papers in order, but when the clutter has been eliminated and the systems for keeping them in order have been set up, they should be much easier to handle.

Borrowing Ideas from Business Consultants

One specialist says the clutter is not on your desk (or in your cupboards, drawers, or closets). It is in your mind. We spend a good bit of our time looking for things that should be readily accessible. We live with a lot of frustration because of this.

This expert recommends that all incoming papers be handled in one of four ways: (1) they should be dropped straight into the garbage can; (2) they should be delayed for further action—like bill-paying day; (3) they should be delegated to someone else to handle—the bill payer or your children; (4) they should be dealt with on the spot. Try never to put down a piece of paper without making a decision about it.

Learn to open the mail beside the garbage can. If you must open direct mail pieces, make a quick decision about whatever it is the piece offers and then either put the order form and return envelope in a place to be dealt with later or toss the whole lot. It's all right to toss unopened direct mail pieces!

Sometimes we cannot act on something because it upsets us. Sometimes we have to wait for more information before we can deal with a piece of paper. Sometimes we simply don't know what we are going to do with that piece of paper. Sometimes we don't want to toss it, but it has low priority. And sometimes we just plain want to procrastinate. We have to devise a system to store pieces of paper until we can deal with them. Maybe several open-topped boxes on a shelf will suffice.

If mail comes for your children, have a specific mail pickup spot. This becomes more important as they get older and are sometimes living at home and sometimes not.

Deal with as much paper as you can on the spot. If incoming mail requires an answer, try to answer it immediately. Sometimes a note can be written at the bottom of a letter and the original letter sent back. Drop notes or postcards as responses to letters. Make necessary phone calls as soon as possible.

A tip in a business publication says to scan magazines, tear out what is useful or of interest, and toss the remainder of the magazine away. Keep the article, filed by subject, until you have time to read it or need the information. Don't even read the rest of the magazine. If the whole magazine is of value, file it somewhere accessible. Some magazine companies have binders for this purpose, and some companies provide yearly indexing for quick reference.

What to Do with Your Children's Papers

It would take only a few years to completely fill a house with your children's "important papers." To some children everything is important and they refuse to part with any paper carried home from school, church, scouting, and club programs. Some children like to collect napkins and menus from restaurants, gum wrappers from who knows where, pictures, posters, packaging materials from their favorite fast-food restaurants, and all kinds of stuff.

What do you do with it all? You can sweep into the child's territory with a shovel and a wastebasket and ruthlessly swoosh it all out the door, but that really upsets some children and only makes them more determined to keep their clutter safe from invading moms.

Alice Skelsey has an excellent idea for eliminating this paper clutter. It is a Me Box. Each member of the family, or at least each child, has a Me Box. It is a place where pieces of paper and other "valuables" can be placed until a later time when they are evaluated (by the child) for saving or tossing. Into this box can go his best pictures from school, his perfect test papers, birthday cards, photos, report cards, postcards from favorite places, and anything else he chooses to put there.

The box need be nothing more than a stationery or envelope box with a lid. It should be labeled with the child's name and the year. You can also use Christmas gift boxes, which are a little larger than an envelope box and may be very attractive as well. Or you can purchase decorative storage boxes.

Twelve of these boxes, one for each school year, would make only a small pile—small enough to be stored on a closet shelf. It is a fortunate child who has a Me Box. About once a year, maybe at the end of a school year, the child should go through the contents of the box and sort and discard. Then he can keep just those treasures that have truly lasting value to him. Perhaps he will consolidate the contents of the boxes so he will not have twelve at the end of his school years, but only six or eight.

It is possible to be organized but you must be committed to it. If you begin to let things go, you may become overwhelmed with the demands on your time and the clutter in your home.

11

But i Need it Tomorrow!

It's 8:30 P.M. At last you've sunk down in your favorite chair to relax.

"Billy," you call out to one of your children. "Have you done your homework?"

"Yeah. Oh, no! I forgot I have to have a report on Greenland to turn in tomorrow. I have to go to the library, right now! Can you take me, Mom? Dad?"

"Well, Billy, you've really got a problem. The library closed half an hour ago."

That is a common scene in many households. It happens night after night in homes all around the country. Even if the library had been open, running Billy over there is time-consuming. It is at least as time-consuming as running to the grocery store for one ingredient for a cake or to the auto-parts store for an oil filter when changing the oil. Extra trips take extra time, and our goal should be to find ways to save time and to make more efficient use of our time.

The library junket could have been planned as a family outing when every member of the family goes to look for books, videos, music tapes, and CDs, and a host of other things libraries provide while Billy is searching for the material he needs. It could have been used as training in how to use the library's tools and facilities for other members of the family. But because it happened unplanned (and it always will with children), it was only a source of frustration for parents and child.

All kinds of things are suddenly needed for tomorrow. Information for homework reports may be the leading instant need, and for families who have access to the Internet at home, this may not be as big a problem as it used to be. But sometimes the need is a costume a child conveniently forgot to tell you about or supplies for a school project.

One thing that will help save the time and frustration that comes from trying to find information for a report at the last minute is to own some basic reference books. These would be a set of encyclopedias, an atlas, a good dictionary, and perhaps some books about various cultures and countries of the world. I have also found it valuable to own a few volumes of poetry. The most useful are those that include the works of a number of writers rather than just one.

Building a Reference File

Why not help your child build a ready reference file of current information? Save and file articles on and pictures of various foreign countries, animals, family activities, and so on. Think about the needs your children have had for resource materials in the last few years, and build your resource file to meet those needs. A great resource for filling these files is *National Geographic* magazine. These magazines are available at thrift shops, garage sales, and from friends who hate to throw them out but don't know what to do with them. When the *National Geographic* features a country, it will often insert a map of that country. These are a great resource. Be careful, though, that you store only up-to-date materials. For instance, out-of-date maps should be discarded and replaced with new ones.

You may want to have a file of just pictures, since children are always needing a picture of something or other. Save attractive pictures from magazines, greeting cards, calendars, and advertisements. When you see one, clip it out and drop it in the file. Involve your children in the process. They will enjoy cutting out pictures and learning how to file them. They will also enjoy going to this file later on and just browsing through it for fun. (You may enjoy it, too.)

Add to this file free information the child can send for through the mail. There are lists of sources for this material in the back of any regional or travel publication.

When you are out and about, traveling or sight-seeing, watch for booklets, pamphlets, maps, postcards, and prints from art galleries. All of these can be added to the file.

Building a home reference library file can be a fun project for the whole family to work on together. Before long, everything you or your children pick up will be evaluated as a possibility for the file, and soon everyone in the family will be helping to build it. The problem then may be that your filing cabinet is too small.

If the children are old enough, show them how to file the folders alphabetically. They will be learning some basic organizational skills. Children too young to read can find their way around in the file if you place a symbol or a picture of what is inside on the file so they can identify it.

A Supply of Supplies

It is time-consuming to run to the store for all the little bits and pieces needed to complete a school project. Begin to build a supply of 3″ x 5″ file cards, tape, scissors, folders, rulers, staples, liquid correction fluid, glue and glue sticks, spray adhesive glue, colored paper, white paper, pencils, felt-tipped markers, ribbon, wrapping paper, tissue paper in colors, razor blades and Exacto knives (for you to use in helping them), poster board, and anything else that would be useful in putting together projects for school.

Build your supply slowly so that you don't go bankrupt. Watch for office store specials and check for useful items on their closeout tables. Just remember, you are making an investment in your children and at the same time saving yourself many trips to the store.

Building a Costume Resource

It seems that several times a year children arrive home to announce their need of a costume—tomorrow! Nothing can be more frustrating to a parent than to be faced with the prospect of making a costume in a hurry.

You can, however, build a costume resource. Our big trunk had everything we ever thought could be useful for a costume. Here is a list of some basic items that are useful in building a costume resource and some ideas for using them:

Satiny robes for kings' robes or wise men's costumes

Long dresses for antebellum ladies, queens, or just for pretend

Cloaks and shawls for turn-of-the-century characters or Sherlock Holmes, detectives, sinister villains, and other mysterious people

A lab technician's coat

Sheets for angels, wedding dresses, and trains on royal clothing

Ruffled blouses and men's evening shirts with ruffles

Tights in all colors

Long, brightly colored skirts for ethnic costumes

White aprons for Raggedy Ann, maid's costumes, and mothers' attire

Loud plaid jackets are great for clowns

Big wide belts and sashes

Beads, rings, gaudy brooches

Bits of lace, collars, pieces of fur, fur prints, yardage with ethnic prints

Raincoats and ponchos in all colors

Hats of all kinds

Vests, unusual boots and shoes, purses, canes, and umbrellas with unusual colors or handles

Wigs (get the washable kind so they can be thoroughly cleaned)

Lace curtains and tablecloths, netting, and tulle can all be worked into spectacular costumes

Old glasses frames and spectacles

If you can find the time to put only one idea from this chapter into use, I hope you will choose to set up a costume trunk. It's lots of fun for the whole family, and it will save you the time of running to fabric stores, costume shops, and other places for supplies. The costumes don't have to be saved just for school events. Every once in a while use them for dressing up on Family Night.

Working Ahead

While you're at it, why not prepare ahead for other upcoming family events?

One year from your child's birthday this year, she'll have another one. You'll probably want to have pretty paper plates, tablecloths, hats, and other birthday paraphernalia. Why not take some time and buy all at once the party supplies for your children's birthdays next year? Put them away in a special cupboard to await their special days.

What about other family members and friends? Don't their birthdays come every year without fail? Could you do all your card shopping in one great blitz instead of rushing out at the last minute to buy a card, or forgetting about it altogether? File your cards in a greeting card folder, available in many card shops. Write the day the card should be mailed right where the stamp goes. The stamp will cover your reminder to yourself.

Speaking of stamps, if your time truly is important, buy stamps in bulk and in all the denominations you will use. Nothing is a bigger waste of time than standing in line at a post office.

What about gift wrap, tape, ribbons, gift enclosures, and all those other things we need periodically? Gift wrap is usually on sale the day after Christmas. I try to buy wrap that would be suitable not just for Christmas but for other special occasion days as well.

In the realm of paper products come paper plates, napkins, and cups for daily household and picnic use. Large warehouse shopping centers, where it is possible to buy these items in bulk, have sprung up around the country. It saves money and time to buy in bulk.

If you can afford to buy household paper products in bulk, and if you have a place to store them, do so. It will be months before you reach for the last of them.

Buy school supplies well ahead of the rush. Put them away and don't let eager little hands get into them before schooltime, or you will have wasted both time and money.

All of this will take an initial investment of time to get started, and if you are not used to making time for organization, this could be frustrating. Hang in there. These are just suggestions to think about and implement when you can and only if you really want to. You are the only one who can decide how you want to spend your time.

The goal of this chapter has been to help you always be prepared, to free you from the tyranny of the urgent cry, "I need it tomorrow," and to help your children learn how to organize materials in such a way as to be retrievable and useful to them.

12

What's for Dinner? and Similar Questions

I'm not the kind of person who lives to eat. I buy food because I have to. I cook it because it is necessary. I'm not particularly fond of cleaning up after a meal but I don't suppose that's unique.

Even though cooking doesn't excite me a whole lot, I am fascinated by various systems women devise and use for the time management of meal planning, food purchasing, and food preparation. I have been collecting these ideas for years. I'll share some of the better ideas here as starting points for you to develop your own system.

Keeping a Menu File

Idea #1. All of my well-organized friends keep menu files for meal planning. There are many ways to do this. Some of these women, working outside their home, keep their menus in daily planners right alongside their business appointments. They also list items there that they might need to pick up on the way home from work.

Idea #2. One author suggests keeping menu files on just four to six cards. On each card are listed all the items that will be used in a single meal. There is also a record of the place where the recipe for each dish can be found. These four to six cards are rotated from week to week with a new menu added from time to time.

Four to six dinner menus may not be enough variety for your family. Maybe eight to twelve would be less predictable, especially if they were not rotated in the same order each time, so that pot roast one day is not always followed by pizza the next.

What's nice about this system is that these cards can be pulled and checked against your master shopping list to see if you have all the ingredients on hand or if you will need to buy some items.

Idea #3. Another woman puts every dish of the meal on a separate card. These she mixes and matches into interesting meal combinations. She recommends updating and adding to this file, but only with family-taste-tested recipes.

Idea #4. I have used several systems, but the one I like best is a card system set up by main entrée for the evening meal. Group cards under beef, chicken, ham, eggs, cheese, casseroles. On each card is not only the type of meat, but also how it is to be prepared (baked chicken, fried ham, and so forth). The card also lists the vegetables, salad, and other accompaniments to the meal, all the way down to beverages and condiments. I also include either the recipe or the location of the recipe so that no time is wasted looking for it.

At one time I had a pocket system into which the week's cards were placed. On a small piece of tagboard, I made pockets that were simply number 10 envelopes cut in half and glued on. There was one for each day of the week.

The day before I went shopping, I pulled from the file box the menu cards I wanted for the week. My choices were sometimes governed by the kind of meat being offered on sale that week. If beef was on sale, I went first to the beef section of my menu box and decided which beef recipes I would use. I made my shopping list from the cards, then placed the cards in the appropriate weekday pockets.

For example:

In the Sunday pocket would go:

Five-hour pot roast of beef (recipe on back)

potatoes

carrots

onions

Green salad

Gelatin dessert and cookies

Beverages

milk

tea

At the same time I was thinking about which menus to use, I was planning to buy a pot roast large enough so that there would be some left for another meal later in the week when I would be too busy to cook. (More about that later.)

This could be an excellent way to get some help in starting dinner. Often family members don't help because they don't know what the plan is. With just a few instructions given ahead of time, a junior high student could make a salad, a husband could put the roast in the oven, and a child could set the table.

There is one thing to consider when planning your menus: No matter which system you use, include the five basic categories of foods, which are not, as a friend of mine once said, "Green, brown, white, yellow, and glop," but rather protein (meat, poultry, fish, dry beans, eggs, and nuts), dairy (milk, cheese, yogurt), grain products (bread, rice, pasta, cereals), fruits, and vegetables. Remember, the bulk of your family's diet should come from the vegetable, fruit, and grain groups.

Double-Up Cooking

A number of years ago, I read about a system called DOLODOL cooking. These seven letters were applied to the days of the week so that *D*s landed on Sunday and Thursday. *O*s fell on Monday, Wednesday, and Friday. *L*s were on Tuesday and Saturday.

The *D* in the formula stood for "double" cooking days, the *O* was for "only one," and the *L*s were for leftover days. On the "only one" days, the cook prepared just enough food for one meal—nothing left over.

You may not want to stick to this formula exactly but if you cook double a couple of days a week, you'll have a couple of days when you won't have to cook. Just put the extra amount in the freezer for another time, perhaps to be used another week.

It is great to come in from work, reach in the freezer for a ready meal, and pop it in the oven. Add a salad or a vegetable, and dinner is ready.

Another double-up idea is to cook a rather large turkey—sixteen or eighteen pounds. When I did this, after the first meal, I would completely bone the turkey and package it in family-sized portions to be used later on. I detest boning a turkey. It makes such a mess. But I loved being able to reach into the freezer for a package of turkey and know that by laying slices of white turkey meat over cooked broccoli, adding a Mornay sauce, popping the whole lot into the oven for forty minutes (a lot less in a microwave), toasting some French bread, and pouring the beverages, dinner could be ready in no time.

Grocery Shopping

It is more economical to buy one large cut of beef for roasting than two small ones. A large cut provides not only meat for the first meal but also sliced meat for sandwiches and bits and pieces for stew and other dishes. The juices are good for making gravy or soup stock. If there is a bone in the meat, it can be boiled with celery leaves, herbs, onions, and garlic to make wonderful soup stock.

Buying larger is not only more economical but it also saves time. If you have the space to store extra food, it is wise to buy a quantity of staple items or at least large packages. Remember, fewer trips to the store means more time for family fun.

The idea behind bulk buying is to never be without something you will need, whether it is a food item or some other commodity normally purchased in a grocery store.

The ideal would be that if a child asks for toothpaste, you have an extra tube on the shelf. If someone breaks his shoelace, you have an extra pair on hand. If you want to bake a cake, you have all the necessary ingredients. You may never reach this ideal but perhaps you could do better than you are doing now.

Create a Master Shopping List

How can anyone function without a grocery shopping list? I suppose you can just go to the store and buy whatever you remember that you need. Some people have better memories than others and shopping this way works for them, but most of us need help and we end up making repeated trips to the store for items we forgot and spending more money than we intended, if we don't use a list.

A master shopping list is the most efficient way to shop. It lists items in the order you find them in your favorite grocery store. During the week, as you run out of items or plan meals, simply circle the things you need on the master list.

It takes a little work to get started. It is helpful if your supermarket has a floor plan that gives the layout of the store in detail. If not, go through the store, following your usual route, and jot down main categories of items along the way: produce, deli, canned vegetables, soups, condiments, paper products, bakery goods, and so on. Don't forget the ends of the aisles and the hidden corners of the stores. When you get home you can fill out your list with the particular items your family uses. You might list in the condiments section salad dressings, mayonnaise, barbecue sauce, ketchup, mustard, and relish.

If you have a computer, store the list there. Then you can easily update it and print out copies whenever they're needed. If you don't have access to a computer, get the list typed. If you don't type, barter something for a typist's time. Get a couple of copies of the list and test it to see if you forgot anything and if the list is going to work well for you. Then, when the list is the way you want it, duplicate a supply. Post one on the refrigerator or elsewhere in your kitchen, and every time you or anyone else in the family uses the last item in stock, circle it on the master list. If everyone does this, getting ready for a shopping trip will be easy.

The night before your shopping trip, sit down with your supermarket's food ad and see what is being offered as a seasonal or money-saving special. Just two words about trying to save money by shopping multiple stores: *You won't.* Over a period of time, each store will offer a sale on most of the items your family will need. They won't all be offered in the same week, but if you plan your buying and buy the special items in quantity, you will reap about the same financial savings as you would if you shopped several stores and you'll realize a big savings in shopping time. Who wants to stand in checkout lines over and over?

Putting It All Away

The time to get everything organized and as nearly ready for cooking as possible is when you are unpacking your groceries. Make meat patties and layer with waxed paper. Freeze enough for a family meal in one plastic bag. One woman I know browns all the ground beef she will be using for cooking during the week. Then the cooled, cooked meat is frozen in individual packages in the amounts in which it will be used. So if she has a recipe that calls for browned ground meat, it's all ready to go. She has used only one cooking pan, done it all at one time right after shopping, and cleaned up splattered grease only one time.

Before freezing a large cut of meat, slice off pieces to use in other meals. Wash and dry all fruits and vegetables. Prepare celery and carrot sticks for munching and store in the refrigerator in plastic bags.

One mother makes all the lunch box sandwiches for the period of time until her next shopping trip. She stores them in the freezer. This is a real time-saver in the mornings when everyone is getting ready to go to work and school. If the sandwiches are ready, all you need to do is grab a brown bag, put in a frozen sandwich, a piece of fruit, and a couple of cookies or a container of yogurt. Remember, mayonnaise does not freeze well.

Other Timesaving Ideas

Set aside days for mass-producing food. Bake two chocolate cakes instead of just one and freeze the extra. Bake lots of cookies or freeze extra dough in unbaked rolls for slicing and baking as needed. Prepare several casseroles at one time. Make your own frozen dinners for the times when there is no cook at your house.

Use your freezer to its maximum capacity. Use it to store bread. A trip to a bakery thrift store can save both time and money and provide your family with a variety of baked goods.

If your family is large, invest in a few large pots and pans. It takes a lot less time to put all the pasta in one pot and cook it than to do it in two batches. It takes a lot less time to fry all the chicken in one oversized electric fry pan than it does to do it twice in a smaller pan.

Buy some freezer-to-oven or microwave containers. It will save you time to be able to use the same container for different purposes.

Good food goes a long way toward keeping people content and happy. Food that is prepared with some prethought as to color and texture looks "good enough to eat."

It doesn't take any longer to cook a good meal than it does to cook a bad one. The difference may only be in the planning.

Making Your Equipment Work for You

There are gadgets for every purpose you can think of and many you have never thought about. It's tempting to invest in them. They look so useful.

But consider for a moment the value of the gadget and what it can do against the time it takes to maintain it and keep it in repair. Dare I suggest that perhaps a gadget's worth is in question when it takes longer to take it apart and clean it than it does to use it? Why buy a fancy salad shredding-and-chopping instrument when a really great quality chef knife will do the same job?

The chopper/shredder has to be taken apart and cleaned. The knife can be wiped off and replaced in the knife holder in about five seconds.

We all need some good basic tools to use in our homes—a good can opener, great knives, a vacuum cleaner, basic garden tools. We need appliances to help us with our work. We need to buy the best appliances we can afford, but we probably don't need to buy top-of-the-line appliances to get the job done. A simpler, less complicated appliance may work as well or better than the expensive model and in the long run may not need costly repairs.

Buy only the conveniences you need in an appliance. Every added convenience is one more thing that can break down. Ask yourself:

1. What do I really need in an appliance?
2. What extra features would save me time and what ones are nice but not needed?
3. How much do the extra features cost?
4. Will the extra features make repair more expensive?
5. Is this appliance easy to clean and care for?

Give some careful and serious thought to the appliances you purchase. Do your homework. Check *Consumer Reports* to see which brand is the best for the money spent. Often it is not the most expensive one.

Young couples starting out with limited funds need to prioritize their purchases. Certainly a washer and dryer become top priority when the first baby comes. A self-defrosting refrigerator can save hours of time and eliminate a messy job. A self-cleaning oven may be a luxury, but how wonderful to not spend half a day with your head in the interior of your oven. A dishwasher is a great help and time-saver, especially if family members can be trained to put their dirty dishes in it instead of on the counter. (I wish you luck.)

A freezer makes it possible to take advantage of special food sales and seasonal fruits and vegetables. It also allows you to stock up and thereby avoid multiple trips to the store. In addition, it helps in the multiple-meals preparation described earlier.

A blender can be a great help and time-saver. It can whirl frozen orange juice into a frothy beverage. It can grate cheese, puree vegetables for baby food, mix sauces and gravy bases, foam hot milk for espresso drinks, and of course, mix all kinds of wonderful beverage concoctions. A blender is a good investment for a family.

A telephone with a long handset cord or a cordless phone can be a great investment in saving time. You can do a lot of things while chatting on the phone if you can move around easily. You can fold clothes or wipe down the fronts of cupboards, reorganize and clean the insides of drawers and cupboards, load or unload the dishwasher. In fact many of the small tasks that fill up our days can be accomplished while talking on the phone.

Make that telephone your best friend by using it to order as much as possible from catalogs, specialty houses, and businesses with delivery service. When you have to go out on an errand, call ahead to be sure the business is open or that the person you want to see is there. Perhaps you can even have the item you want waiting for you when you arrive and thus save even more time. For example, call ahead for a pizza and have it waiting when you arrive. Call the video rental shop and have them set aside the video you want. Ask the dry cleaner to find your cleaning and have it waiting for you. Make sure the car repair place has completed its work before you go by to pick up your car.

Learn to Use Your Equipment

Most people buy an appliance because they think they need it and often they do. They buy it for one needed function, overlooking the fact that the same appliance may be capable of multiple uses. Learn how to use your appliances to get the maximum benefit from them.

Take, for example, a microwave oven. Perhaps there has never been another tool invented that is such a time-saver for busy homemakers. Microwaves are great for cooking "from scratch" meals, cutting the preparation time at least in half.

But how many people do you know who use the microwave only for warming food, making popcorn, or defrosting things? Most microwaves come with an instruction book that gives the basic functions for cooking by microwave.

The cookbook that came with my microwave has seventeen pages of information, tips, and instructions for using the appliance, plus wonderful recipes. The book includes everything from heating or reheating food to working with convenience foods, baking breads, and making sauces and gravies. It also tells how to adapt your favorite recipes for microwave cookery, and there is information on how food cooks in a microwave.

If the purchaser of a new microwave takes the time to read through the manual and completely understand the capabilities of the oven, that person will be able to use the appliance to its greatest capacity. I confess I read through only part of the manual, and I know only part of what the oven will do. (I learned quickly how to make microwave two-minute fudge!)

Companies spend thousands of dollars to make sure your appliances do the best job for you. Then they give you well-researched, well-written manuals to help you get the best results. All of this information is there for your reading. The time invested in learning how to use your appliances will be repaid quickly in timesaving shortcuts.

Buy Survivors

A question frequently asked at our house when our children were helping out was, "Mom, can I put this in the dishwasher?" or "Mom, what will happen if I put this in the microwave?" My standard answer was, "I don't know. Let's find out."

So we would put it in and see if it survived. I didn't want anything in my house that could not survive. I did not want clothing that I had to hand wash, so I inspected labels when purchasing garments to see if they were machine washable.

But what about things like wool sweaters? I wash wool sweaters in the washing machine. As recommended, I use cold water, a good soap for wool, and a short, gentle cycle. The sweaters are never machine dried. Instead, wool sweaters are spread out and blocked to dry. Washing your sweaters saves a lot on dry cleaning bills.

Silk blouses can also be washed in the machine. There is a silk-washing product, or you can use the same gentle wool-washing soap. Here too use a short, gentle cycle. Line dry silks until completely dry. The difficult part of washing silks is ironing them. They almost have to be soaking wet to get the wrinkles out. Drying them completely assures that all the seams are dry. Then spray the rest of the garment with water and iron on the wrong side with a medium setting on the iron.

Here is a rule to remember. *Never put anything away that is not ready to wear.* Perhaps an even better rule is to never put anything into the washing machine that is not ready to wear. Mend small rips and tears before the garment goes into the washer. Those small rips and tears have a way of growing into big rips and tears in the washer. Save hand mending for television viewing time or when assisting a child with homework.

> Never put anything away that is not ready to wear.

When putting away seasonal clothes, give them an extra careful inspection. Have them cleaned so that when the first snowy or warm spring day arrives, you're ready for it. This is a good time to evaluate whether this garment is going to survive another season. Will it be sadly out of style by next year? Will the children have outgrown it, and there's not another child coming along to use it? Did you wear it this season but really hate it? If the answer to any of these questions is yes, get rid of it. Give it to some charity. There may be someone out there who would love it and could be making good use of it. Besides, you don't want to spend money cleaning it and then throw it away when the season changes.

A way to keep from throwing away clothes from one year to the next is to avoid trendy clothing and to stick to classics and basics. Classic suits and dresses will be in style for years. A new blouse, scarf, or jewelry piece will help make them seem new. If you buy good quality shirts, ties, suits, dresses, and children's clothing and if they are properly cared for, they will last for years.

13

Beg, Buy, or Barter Time

Barter for the Help You Need

If you cannot afford to buy the help you need, consider bartering something you can do (secretarial services, accounting, and so on) for something you cannot do (painting, wallpapering, housecleaning, yard work, or changing the oil in your car).

When we were very poor and my son, Mark, wanted to learn to play the viola, I bartered my abilities as a gardener in exchange for lessons for him. Once a week we would go to his teacher's house. He would take an hour-long lesson and I would cut her grass, weed her flower beds, prune her bushes, and thoroughly water everything. It was a win, win, win situation. Mark learned to play the viola, his teacher got her grass cut, and I didn't have to pay. As a bonus, all that exercise kept my weight down.

If you feel you have nothing to barter, try swapping something—like your kids. Now before you're tempted to say, "That's a great idea! Why didn't I think of that myself?" hear me out.

Isn't it true that you find yourself saying, "If I could just work at this without interruption, I could get it finished"? Well, why don't you work out a swap with a friend (this is especially good for singles). You take all the kids one Saturday (hers or his) and he or she takes them all the next. That gives each of you a full day to jump in and tackle some big, heavy-duty tasks without interruption.

Here's a day to clean the garage without the troops hauling everything you throw out back from the garbage can. Or maybe you want to turn some rooms inside out and clean them. Maybe you'd like to paint the bathroom. Perhaps you could say you were going to do all those things and then decide to just sit and listen to the quiet.

Buying Housecleaning

One way to buy time is to hire someone to clean your house. Since many women work outside their home, more and more housecleaning and maid services are springing up around the country. Rates for these services vary and may seem expensive until you measure the time saved against the dollars spent.

In truth, most working women are holding down two jobs—one in the marketplace and another at home. Many working women have little time to play with their family because Saturdays need to be spent doing all the household tasks that can't be done during the week.

Some women hire a housekeeper once a week, others bimonthly, and others seasonally or only when needed. Each household needs to find the level of its need and hire accordingly.

Some people feel uncomfortable about hiring service workers to help them. I'll never forget when I hired my first housekeeper. It was all I could do to keep from cleaning the house before she did, and I'll never forget the guilt I felt. It lasted all of ten minutes, and ever since then I have thoroughly enjoyed having my house cleaned for me.

That doesn't mean I never vacuum a floor or change a bed. Since I have a housekeeper only twice a month, I vacuum, dust, and clean bathrooms on the off week. I also take care of all the laundry. I do, however, leave the heavy cleaning to the housekeeper.

An alternative to going to a commercial housecleaning service is to hire a teenager or several teenagers or college students to help with household and outdoor seasonal tasks. Not long ago, I hired a college student to wash all my windows—twenty-one windows, to be exact. I got them washed for less than I would have had to pay a commercial service, and the student had money to put toward her tuition.

Teach Your Kids to Work

You may think that teaching your kids to work is not a time-saver. It's faster to do it yourself! That may be true in the beginning, but over the long haul, kids can be a great help around the home and ultimately can save you lots of time. Of course, just about the time they are truly a help and are well trained, they leave home.

It is often the case that children don't help because they don't know what needs to be done; they don't know how to do it; they're afraid to try because they are afraid they will fail.

If you're going to teach your child to work, you must, for a moment, step back mentally to his age and think about what you knew and what you did not know about work. Then begin from that point. Cut a large, complex task apart into bite-sized pieces and begin by teaching the way to do each bite-sized piece.

Take, for example, cleaning a room. To say to a child, "Go clean your room," is very discouraging. She hasn't a clue where to begin. You need to work with her the first time or two and say, "First we have to get everything off the floor so we can clean. Let's pick up all the toys and put them where they belong." Then give the child the opportunity to do that. "Good," you might say, "that looks better already. Now let's pick up all the clothes and hang them up." (I'm assuming the hooks and rods in her closet are the right height for her to do what you've asked.)

"Now that we have everything put away, we can go on. Here's a dustcloth and this is how we use it." Show the child how to dust the furniture. Show her how to make the bed. Decide whether or not she is big enough to handle the vacuum cleaner. If she is, show her how to use it. If she is not, decide who will do this for her.

Every job you give a child should have a beginning and an end. It should be short enough to be within her attention span. Sometimes a challenge helps. There is something about working toward a goal that is encouraging. How much do you think you can do in fifteen minutes? Do you think you can clean your whole room in half an hour?

When the task is finished, let the child tell you how she did. Let her evaluate her work. Resist the impulse to pick her work to pieces. Remember that if you want her to try again, she needs to be encouraged, not discouraged. And you do want her to try again! A written checklist can be a helpful evaluation tool. Let her go over the checklist to see if she did everything that needed to be done.

When your children are old enough to do major projects, you can hire them to do yard work, wash windows, wash your car, and so on. For some families, this is successful. I often found that my two worked better for the neighbors than they did for me, even when I paid them the same amount. I couldn't figure out why, but from talking with other parents I found this is just the way kids are.

When you pay your own children, the money you give them stays in the family and therefore saves you money elsewhere down the line. Although children should have regular household tasks that they do just because they live at your house, they can also benefit from being paid. Money is a good incentive for doing work, especially for kids. You can teach them to work while getting the help you need, and you keep the money in the family. Everyone profits.

Work assignments should be geared to children's age level. As much as possible, give them an entire project to do and the instructions for how you want it done and then get out of the way and let them do it. Treat them with dignity, as you would if you were hiring an outsider to do the job.

Part-Time Work

If you work outside the home, you may find that working part-time is an option for you. This may give you the income you need and allow you to stay involved in your field but also afford you a few more hours to be at home. Mats Brenner, a mathematician from Bloomington, Minnesota, has decided part-time work is best for his family. Mats works for Honeywell just four days a week. The rest of the week he plays with his kids. Mary, his wife, also works four days a week at Honeywell as a scientist.

"I view it [part-time work] as a viable way to work and advance, while still finding time for other pursuits, most recently, caring for my children," says Charlene Canape, wife, mother of two children, writer, and former editor of *Business Week,* in her book *The Part-time Solution.*[4]

Often part-time working mothers are more content with their lives than other working women. Although it is possible to work full-time at a career and manage to keep up with everything else, one needs to ask the questions, Is it worth the struggle? Could there be another way? Part-time work for one or both parents can be a solution with happy results. There are advantages and disadvantages to part-time work, and both men and women need to look at them.

Advantages

Part-time work gives you more hours at home, since part-time can mean anything from ten to thirty-nine hours a week. Most part-time jobs are twenty to thirty hours a week. There are all kinds of ways to put these hours together. A great advantage can be gained if the hours can be bunched together on set days, rather than spreading a few hours a day throughout a work-week. Three eight-hour days will probably give you more time at home than five four-and-one-half-hour days, simply because you have to get ready and commute to work only three times, rather than five. However you put it together, twenty-four hours of employment rather than forty is going to give you more time at home.

Part-time work gives you more energy to work at home. Less commuting and less stress are bound to give you more energy. Often the kind of work done at home is different from your employment, and the change can be energizing.

Part-time work gives independence. While their children are young, many women do not want to return to full-time jobs. At the same time, they may have become used to having their own money and making decisions about how to spend that money. They enjoy working but they also want to be at home to meet their children's needs. For many, this dilemma can be solved by working part-time.

Child care arrangements may be easier for part-time workers. In some part-time situations, parents may be able to arrange their schedules in such a way that child care is covered by the flexibility of both parents' schedules. If it is not, it may be easier to find someone to care for the child a few days a week or a few hours a day than it is to find a caretaker for a full workweek.

Part-time work provides a way to experiment with occupations. Part-time work provides both teenagers and parents with an opportunity to see what jobs are available and how they might fit into those jobs. Part-time work can give you the opportunity to look for a different or more rewarding type of work.

> Use part-time work to experiment with occupations.

It used to be that people trained for a job and stayed in it for the rest of their life, but that is not the case today. Now people may retrain four or five times and start new careers at any time. It's part of what makes being alive today so great! If you hate your job, do something else. Retrain! Rethink your whole approach to work! Start your own business!

Part-time work is a way to maintain Social Security and other benefits. Many women, who don't want to work full-time, work part-time just to maintain their Social Security or benefits from the company where they have been previously employed.

Part-time work can provide an escape from routine housework. A part-time job can get you out of the house for a few hours a week and thereby break the monotony. The only problem is that many part-time jobs are also monotonous. Take a good look before you leap.

Disadvantages

There are also some disadvantages to be weighed in all of this. *Part-time jobs don't pay much,* unless your line of work is highly skilled and there is great demand for it. It is wise, as in all jobs, to weigh what you will get in income against what it will cost you to work—clothes, child care, transportation, social obligations, and so forth.

Part-time employment is on the rise, and one of the reasons is that *if employees work under a certain number of hours, employers don't have to pay benefits.* With the high cost of benefits, many employers are hiring multiple part-timers and still getting their work done. If benefits are important to you, this is something to consider.

Your own attitude can work against you. An attitude that says, "I'm only a part-timer, so therefore I should be able to do my housework and yardwork without any help," opens the possibility of your coming under enough stress to sink the ship. If you work part-time, you are still a working person, with all the stresses accompanying that role.

You do need help. You need help at least from your family. You may need help from a nanny, a housekeeper, or a gardener. You may also need a break from your children, the same way your full-time working sisters and brothers do. It is possible, if you cultivate an attitude in which you fail to take care of yourself, to end up more worn-out than a full-time worker.

Other Things to Consider

If you decide that part-time work is the way for you and your family to go, here are some more points to consider:

1. Decide which hours of the week would be best for you to work. As long as you'll be working part-time, you may as well try to find a job that best fits into your schedule.

2. When deciding hours, think about child care factors. Is there a way to juggle child care so that you can hang on to some of the money you make and not pay it all to a day care center?

3. Are you a morning or an evening person? Could you find a job that fits in with your makeup? Do you want to give your best hours to your job or to your family? When you've answered these questions, start looking for a job you can do during your prime time—the time when you are most awake, most productive, most efficient. Or save the prime time for your family and find a job that doesn't take the best of you.

4. Do you want to work a little every day or a couple of full days? Do you want to get ready to go to work and commute in traffic every day or could you go to work two or three days a week and be just as happy?

is Working at Home the Answer?

There is a strong trend today to work at home. The trend has, in part, been created by electronic technology. When an employee plugs a modem into a computer and a phone line, the ability to communicate with others online is the same as if she were in the company's building. A fax machine makes it possible to see a document almost as quickly as if you walked down the hall to a colleague's office. With e-mail you can have instant communication no matter where you are. I don't know about your office, but in the ones where I have worked, workers e-mail each other even if they are only twenty feet away, so it makes little difference if you are twenty or more miles away.

At-home workstations are becoming more evident.

Large corporations realize their employees produce more work of better quality when they are not distracted by conversation, ringing telephones, drop-of-the-hat meetings, coffee breaks, and so forth. They also know that their employees are going to produce better work if they don't have to spend hours on the freeway or in a train, commuting to and from work. Thus the trend to at-home workstations is becoming more and more evident.

That's one way of working at home, but there are others. Many small businesses are begun in homes to keep overhead costs down. Do not get the mistaken idea that these are part-time jobs. They can be all-consuming in terms of time and energy. Getting a small business launched is probably one of the most taxing ventures anyone can set out to do. You don't establish a home-based business to make big money, either. In the beginning there is little money. Often the owner of the business is fortunate to get any salary at all. Cash flow is a problem that may continue to haunt a small business for many years. However, if a home-based business is to succeed, it has to become profitable sooner or later, and sooner is much better than later.

Some types of home-based businesses are word processing, insurance claim work, editing, writing, child care, home beauty shops, mail-order work, consulting, and photography. My book *101 Ways to Make Money at Home* will give you lots of ideas for starting a home business.[5]

There are important points to consider before starting a home-based business. Find a place to work that can be dedicated strictly to that function. You need a place to spread out your projects and not have to pick them up at the end of every day. It would be great if that room had a door with a lock.

Avoid distractions. It's easy to be distracted by housework and projects around the house. "Well, I'll just stick a load of clothes in the washer. It will only take another minute or so to load the dishwasher." Before you know it, your time is all eaten away.

Prepare for isolation. Recently I talked with a writer friend who had gone home several years ago to freelance. "How's it going?" I asked.

"Oh, Gwen, I just couldn't stand the isolation any longer. I've gone back to work in an editorial office."

I understood, for I had just gone through the longest, darkest winter of my life, one in which the isolation nearly incapacitated me. I learned that working out of your home may be all right for some people to do occasionally. For other people, it may even be all right to do every day. But I learned that I need people.

Decide how many hours a week you can work. Can you put in a full workweek from your home? Will you be able to discipline yourself to stay at it that many hours a day?

Count the costs of setting up. Equipment is expensive. Just what will you need, and how much will it cost?

How much can you afford to lose? What if it doesn't work out and you lose money on your home-based business? What happens if you become ill? Can you survive until you are strong enough to work again?

Check out insurance needs. Can you get health insurance that is adequate to your needs if you are self-employed? What will it cost you?

Think about who's going to take care of the business side of your business. Who's going to fill out the legal and tax forms? Do you need an accountant? a lawyer? You probably need both.

What do you need in salary? If you are freelancing for a company other than your own, you probably won't be paid a salary, but will be paid either by the project or on an hourly basis. Will that work for you? If you are paid by the project, do you need to set it up so that part of your earnings come in at the beginning, part in the middle, and part at the end of the project?

Pay attention, and don't be misled by work-at-home scams. There are all kinds of people promising all kinds of things for home-based businesses. Usually they want you to buy some kind of kit or make some kind of investment (often sizable) to start your business. *Be careful!*

Ideas for Saving Time

The following is a list of timesaving tips gleaned from hundreds of sources over many years.

1. Make use of available services—housekeepers, window washers, carpet cleaners, gardening firms.
2. Eliminate things that create work—knickknacks, house-plants, extra clothes, silverware that must be polished, boats, camp trailers, cottages.
3. Try to avoid cooking a hot meal every night of the week.
4. Use the local delicatessen and salad bars in grocery stores.
5. Use as many semiprepared foods as possible.
6. Store equipment near to where it is used.
7. Buy duplicate sets of equipment that you use in different parts of the house.
8. Buy a long extension cord for your vacuum cleaner so you don't have to keep moving the plug to another outlet. Have a cord long enough to reach the entire house.
9. Dovetail jobs—empty the dishwasher and set the table for the next meal at the same time.

10. Plan meals while cleaning the refrigerator or making the weekly shopping list.

11. Teach your children how to cook.

12. Work all the way through a project if possible. It is a time waster to have to restudy or rethink a project.

13. Cut down on overcommunication—too much talk.

14. Keep a book or small project with you for those found moments.

15. Use commute time for learning. Listen to cassette tapes.

16. Use commute time for making phone calls with a cellular phone.

17. Use commute time for thinking and planning. A handheld dictating machine is helpful.

18. Move closer to work to save commuting time or work out of your home if possible.

19. Group phone calls and make a batch of them at one time.

20. Write *short* letters and notes.

21. Read smart—not fast. You don't have to read everything that comes to you. Choose only those items that really interest you or you need to know.

22. Hang up permanent-press clothes as soon as they come out of the dryer.

23. Plan what you are going to wear to work for the entire week. Make sure everything is clean, pressed, and ready to wear. Select shoes, hose, jewelry, and so on.

24. Buy a large supply of underwear and socks so family members run out less frequently.

25. Soak cooking pots and dishes in hot, soapy water as soon as they come from the table. This keeps food from sticking and speeds up cleanup time.

26. When purchasing frequently used items—toothpaste, deodorant, tissues—buy several at one time. Buy for the next two or three months.

27. Organize your cooking utensils. There are dozens of shelving, hanging, and stacking systems to make this an easy task.

28. Lay out your children's clothing if they need help or encourage them to do it themselves.

29. Always put your keys in the same spot, so you never have to look for them.

30. Learn to take time for just doing nothing. It is a valid use of time that often brings renewed creativity.

31. Learn to work with your internal time clock—and those of the other members of your family. Some people are not morning people, and to try to force them to function well in the morning doesn't work. Some people turn into pumpkins by 10:00 P.M. or earlier. People function best when working with, not against, their own time clocks.

32. Ask your friends not to drop by without notice. Tell them you want to see them and give them quality time and since your days are so busy, you can do that only if you know beforehand that they are coming.

33. Keep some simple desserts (cookies, frozen pastries) on hand for those times when friends do come to see you. You may have to hide these deep in the heart of the freezer or in the back of a cupboard.

34. Have a home-repair, do-all-the-little-things day periodically. This is the day for repairmen to come and deliveries to be made. You have to stay home only one day and have it all taken care of at once.

35. Remember, most time is wasted in minutes—not hours.

36. Take full advantage of bank services. Let your bank pay your bills through automatic transfer. To avoid overdrafts when the bill gets to the bank before your income does, arrange for overdraft protection.

37. Have your company automatically deposit your check.

38. Have automatic withdrawals made for savings.

39. Have all of your financial dealings handled by one bank— house payment, car payment, and so on.

40. Have only one or two credit cards and only one or two bills to pay.

41. Buy postage stamps by phone and charge to your credit card. The number is 800-STAMP24.

42. Use only one pharmacy for drugs and prescriptions. Find one that keeps all records on computer and from which you can order refills by phone. At tax time the pharmacy can give you a printout of drug purchases for the year.

43. Look for businesses that offer fast service—ten-minute lube jobs, one-day shirt services, one-hour dry cleaning, places that do quick sewing repairs, mobile services that come to your home for pet grooming, car cleanup, and even veterinary services.

44. Shop at places that feature home delivery.

45. Set time goals for yourself. Think, *The last time I did this it took me half an hour. I wonder if I could do it in twenty minutes this time.* By pushing yourself, you learn to work more efficiently.

46. Work around the room in concentric circles when cleaning rather than crossing back and forth.

47. Separate your summer and winter clothing so you don't have to paw through a clothes rod full of woolens to find a summer blouse or shirt.

48. Take fewer clothes when traveling, especially by air. Plan your wardrobe so everything fits in one carry-on bag. This helps you avoid waiting at the airline's luggage carousel for thirty to forty minutes. You could be well on your way home by that time.

49. Install hooks, racks, and stackable shelving in closets, garages, and cupboards. If things have their own place and if they are in their place, you don't have to look for them, and that could save a lot of time.

50. Keep extra oil in the trunk. It can save you an unscheduled stop at an auto supply store or a service station.

51. Keep in your purse or briefcase a small directory for frequently called phone numbers. Include numbers for any service you might otherwise have to look up in a directory—doctor, dentist, veterinarian, barber or hairstylist, paint store, auto supply store.

52. Hang up your clothes and teach your kids (try, anyway) to hang up their clothes when they take them off, if they are not dirty.

53. Time your jobs and find out how long they really take. If it takes you only five minutes to unload the dishwasher and you know that, you will be less apt to procrastinate about it.

54. Have a gift drawer. Buy gifts on sale and have a ready supply for different occasions. It can be just as special to pick something from your gift drawer as to go to a store and buy it. This is a real time-saver.

55. Have gift wrap, tape, and cards all in one place. Keep a good supply of these on hand.

56. Every time you go to another area of your home—house to garage, for example—look to see what needs to be taken in that direction.

57. Buy long-life light bulbs to avoid having to change them frequently. These are especially good for hard-to-reach places.

58. Label the fuse box or breaker panel to save the time of checking every fuse when one blows out or wondering which breaker is for a certain appliance.

59. Number storm windows and screens so that reinstallation of either will be simple. Use a system such as "DB–1" for "downstairs bedroom, window one."

60. If you do not have an automatic icemaker, make ice cubes in trays and dump them into plastic bags. Then they'll be ready when you need them.

61. Hang garments of one kind together on the closet rod—suits, shirts, dresses, and so forth, and group by color.

62. Pay your bills twice a month. On one of those days, balance your checkbook as well.

63. Do the least-liked tasks from your to-do list first. Everything will be downhill from there.

64. Keep a shopping list on the refrigerator door and train your family to write down an item when they take the last one. Then a quick check through the cupboard and refrigerator on shopping day is all you'll need to be ready for the trip.

65. Keep a big calendar by the phone and write everyone's activities and scheduled events on it. Train the other family members to do the same.

66. If you do not have a dishwasher, allow the dishes to air dry. If you can't get them all in one drainer, buy two.

67. Make the bed the minute you get up and pick up any dropped clothing.

68. Try to make one side of the bed completely before you make the other. Hotel maids and attendants in hospitals do this.

69. Pick different colors of sheets for different sizes of beds so you don't have to search through all your sheets for the right size.

70. Shop when stores are emptiest—early morning or late at night. You could even shop in the middle of the night in a twenty-four-hour store.

71. Get your kids to help with the shopping. Send them in one direction while you go in another. This will work if you have trained them to shop.

72. If you are planning a new house, put the washing machine and dryer near the bedrooms, where the most linen accumulates.

73. Have a laundry basket for each person in the family. Put his or her clean clothes in it and give it to each person to put away.

74. Use TV viewing time for mending, folding clothes, or ironing.

75. Do one major household task each day.

How to Spend the Time You Save

Family Fun Ideas for All Ages

Now that you've discovered how to have more time, use that time for doing fun activities with your family. Here are some ideas.

Preschoolers

Finger plays and other movement. You can find books that give simple ideas for finger plays for small children such as the old, familiar, "This little pig went to market." Start with some ideas from the books and then together, you and your child can make up your own finger play activities.

Put on some music and do rhythm and action movements with your little ones. There are many records available for this kind of activity. Get down on the floor—to their level—and participate with them. Let them show you what the music is telling them to do, and do it with them.

Use your fingers for puppets by painting faces on them and adding little hats and wigs. Then tell a simple story. Paint faces on the children's fingers as well. Let them tell a story. They'll love it.

Face painting. There's a rage, right now, of painting little symbols and flowers on people's faces. This is something a preschool child loves and you don't have to be an artist to please your child. Use eye makeup pencils (which now come in all colors) to do your artwork. A little cold cream will take the makeup off. Hold a mirror down to your child's level so he can see the results.

Nature activities. Gather soft moss and make a dish garden. Use a mirror for a lake, small plants for greens, and tiny figures to decorate the scene. Let the little ones help arrange the figures and decide where trees and lake should go. Don't forget to water the dish garden frequently. It will not last forever, but neither will their interest in it.

Make mud pies or play in the sand with your toddler. If it is snow season, build a snowman together. Get down and get dirty with your child. He or she will love it, and it will be good for you too.

Put up birdhouses and bird feeders close enough to the house so your children can see them. There are some bird feeders that can be attached right to the window. Encourage the children to be quiet and observant when watching the birds. Get a bird book with full-color illustrations so the children can get an up close look at the birds.

Crafts and cooking. Get outdated wallpaper books from a home decorating store. Give them to your preschooler with a pair of blunt scissors and let him cut to his heart's content—or use a catalog or a magazine for the same purpose. You'll have to watch that he doesn't start cutting up every book and magazine. Explain (if he is old enough to understand) that he cannot cut up everything in sight. Put his books for cutting on a low shelf where he can reach them.

Bake bread together. Let the children get involved in kneading the dough, rolling it out, shaping it, and, of course, eating it. Let them taste the various ingredients that make bread: flour, yeast, and extras such as raisins, cinnamon, and sugar.

Little ones can help with mixing up cookies or preparing a casserole. They like to pour already measured ingredients into the bowl. They can stir. Don't worry about a little spilled flour

> Make mud pies or play in the sand with your toddler.

but be sure to supervise closely and don't allow little ones to work near a stove.

Books. Check at your local library to see what they offer for this age group. Many libraries have supervised story hours.

Little ones enjoy simple riddles. Find a book of riddles at the library.

School-Age Children

Crafts. Spend an evening making masks. These can be as simple as a brown paper bag with holes cut for eyes, or papier-mâché creations. Find instructions for how to make masks at your local library or bookstore. Be sure to take pictures of all the creations. They'll provide lots of laughs later in life.

Use aluminum foil to shape various kinds of figures. The foil holds its shape well and is clean and easy to use.

Help your child do a wax resist painting. First cover a piece of art paper with all colors of crayon, good and thick. Then cover the colors with black crayon. Depending on the child's age, you might have to help him so he doesn't get discouraged with the project. Then let him draw his picture by scraping off the black and down to the color with a spoon edge. The effect is a rainbow-colored picture under black. Add a simple mat, available at the art store, and hang his painting somewhere in your house.

Baking and cooking. Build a gingerbread house together. Most cookbooks have information for making gingerbread. Provide lots of frosting, candies, and decorative sprinkles. Don't worry if the outcome looks little like a house and don't worry if many of the decorations disappear into mouths along the way. Help the kids and let them decide what is beautiful.

Let your child plan a full meal for the family. Take him shopping for the food he wants. Give him the money to buy the food and pay for it at the checkout stand. Help him cook and serve the meal—any way he wishes. Encourage his creativity. Do not allow other family members to tease or disparage the child's efforts.

Fun excursions. Go to a beach or a lakeside and build a sand castle. Take along a shovel to move the sand, a funnel for turret tops, and cans to construct towers and roll roadways. In some areas, sand castle building has become a tourist attraction with stiff competition. If you live near such a competition, try to attend and see the wonderful fantasy castles the competitors build.

Visit a bakery or several kinds of bakeries. In-store bakeries in supermarkets often offer kids a cookie credit card they can use when shopping with Mom. It entitles them to one free cookie per visit.

Take a train trip with your school-age child. You don't have to go far, maybe just to the next town and back. Arrange a time when you can eat in the dining car. Sit in the dome car and view the scenery. There is nothing quite like train travel.

Visit a radio or TV station. You can attend the taping of a local show or just view the different processes of a station through windows. When you get home, let your children write a script and record their performance with a cassette player or a video camera.

Other fun things to do. Set up a backyard golf course, using empty coffee cans, croquet wickets, and the natural terrain. Get a couple of golf clubs and some balls and have a crazy playtime together.

Celebrate a birthday the way you would in a foreign country. Get mail-order catalogs from foreign countries or from specialty houses that feature imports. Visit an import store. Get a book from the library on the subject or invite people of different nationalities who may live in your area to tell you about their birthday celebrations.

Teens

Fun places to go. Spend an evening window-shopping for a new car. Go to several car dealerships or visit an automobile show. Talk about how much money it takes for a down payment, how long it takes to pay for a car, and anything else that will give your teen information for a future car purchase.

Go with your teens to a rock concert. It will give you a whole different understanding of this activity. Talk with your teens about the music and lyrics you have heard (if, indeed, you can

> Take a train trip with your school-age child.

still hear when it ends). Even if the type of concert they have chosen is not what you would have picked, closeness can develop from your interest in their activities and music and from talking together about it.

Go on a camping trip with your teens. Pick a place where they can plug in their hair dryers, swim, fly kites, ride bikes, hike, and shop in small towns. Take along some board or card games to play by firelight in the evening. Bring lots of fun foods and snacks. Enjoy!

Go river rafting. Different rivers have different age-level requirements for river running. However, all of them are accessible to teens. River rafting with a professional company is safe and exciting. It is expensive, so make it a very special outing.

Go river rafting with your teens.

Go shopping with your teenager. Give him a set amount of money to spend and encourage him to make it go as far as possible. Then sit back and let him make the decisions about what to buy. If he asks your opinion, give it. If he does not and you know he is making a mistake, let him. It's the best way for him to learn about style and value.

Fun things to learn. Learn something new with your teenager: cross-country or downhill skiing, horseback riding, archery.

Attempt to learn juggling with your teen. Believe it or not, there are books that teach you how to do this. Start out by trying to juggle over a bed. Whatever you are juggling will not fall so far, and you won't have to keep bending over to retrieve it. If you use something like oranges, they will be less likely to break open if they land on a bed.

Fun things to do at home. Rent a video (one they like) and have lots of their friends in for an evening of movies and goodies. Sit down with them and get to know their friends. We did this once and had about sixty-five teenagers crammed into a living room that really could accommodate only about a dozen or so. They had a great time, and it didn't matter that they were packed in so tightly their knees were under their chins.

Let the teens go on a scavenger hunt. Give prizes for the most finds.

Teens might enjoy putting together a video program with friends. Some of their efforts can be very creative. Assist them in their project, perhaps acting as cameraperson or technical assistant. You can send these efforts to national television programs for screening and possible use on programs that use home videos. Let creativity reign and don't underestimate your teen's ability to create a video that will be chosen for nationwide viewing.

Finding Dollars for Family Fun

You can make a little money go a long way. I'm not talking about investing, financial planning, or long-term savings plans. There are lots of books on those subjects. I'm going to tell you how to save money on everyday things and find inexpensive (or free) ways to have fun as a family. If you make your money go a long way, you won't have to work all the time and will still have some money left for doing fun things with your children.

This doesn't involve lowering your quality of life, but expanding it. You don't have to spend a lot of money to eat well, look great, live in a nice house, and drive a decent car. If you are making an average income, all this can be done by learning how to spend money wisely.

I once heard a man say, "Don't always think in terms of satisfying your needs with money. There may be another way to meet them." Over the years I've thought a lot about that statement. At the time I heard it, I was very poor. In time I discovered that the man knew what he was talking about. I learned that fun can be free. I learned that if I helped my friend, she would help me, and both of us would have our needs met without spending money. I learned that because of our nation's affluent lifestyle tons of possessions are given or thrown away every year—good things that could be recycled for my use.

I learned to accept with gratitude what people offered me for free. I learned that they gave it from hearts of love. They wanted me to have it, and if I accepted with a gracious "Thank you," it was enough.

I learned never to look at an object with only its intended purpose in view. Often that item could be used in some other way to meet a need. A lace curtain not only looks beautiful at a window, it can also be used over a colored sheet as a very fancy tablecloth. Brightly colored golf tees can be glued together with wooden beads and other baubles to make colorful, inexpensive Christmas tree ornaments. Wheel rims from cars can be welded together to make stools and table bases for outdoor furniture.

One of the best ways to save money is not to spend it, and one of the ways to avoid spending it needlessly is to take care of the possessions you have.

We've probably all been in homes where children were allowed to be unruly. They may jump on the beds and furniture, write on the walls, throw garbage in the yard, and leave food sitting about. Besides being just plain messy, such misuse of a home and furnishings is expensive.

A sofa and chairs that have been used for a springboard will soon have to be replaced or at least reupholstered—both costly expenditures. Beds that have been used in the same way have to have new mattresses. Spilled food damages carpets and furnishings. It costs money to repaint walls.

We need to consider everything we have as a gift from God. He helps us work for money to buy the things we have, but we are only the caretakers of those things he has loaned us. Most of us cannot live without cash, but

Accept with gratitude what people offer you for free.

if we would learn to "use it up, wear it out, make it do, or do without," we'd have a lot more resources for family fun than we do now.

Some people like to save money. They prepare so well for a rainy day that there is never anything for a sunny today. While it is important to plan for the future, it is also important to live in the present. It's difficult for most of us to achieve balance between spending and saving.

Plan for the future the best you can, but not to the extent that it robs you of the resources for providing quality family times now. At some point we have to trust God with the future, anyway. Why not start now?

Larry Burkett has written extensively on the subject of money and families. Let me summarize some of his ideas. He says God's plan for contentment is:

1. Establish a reasonable standard of living.
2. Establish a habit of giving.
3. Establish priorities.
4. Develop a thankful attitude.
5. Reject a fearful spirit.
6. Seek God's will for you.
7. Stand up to the fear (about money).
8. Trust God's promise.[6]

If we are going to control family saving and spending, we need a plan. That plan has a name that many of us hate—*budget*. In some families a budget becomes the ogre that destroys all fun but it shouldn't. A budget is a plan for spending. It's a tool, not a slave master we serve. Budgets are there to serve us, guide us, and help us have funds for family fun.

Perhaps family values are more apparent in a budget than anywhere else. Each family's goals and priorities are reflected here. One family will value sports events and equipment over every other kind of family activity. Another will spend heavily on books

Everything we have is a gift from God.

and compact discs. Yet others will live in a very simple house and spend their money on travel.

Every family's budget will be different; there is not a right or wrong budget plan. What's right for your family is a plan that takes care of current needs and saves some for the future. We earn money so that we can spend it, and the decisions we make about how to spend it can and should provide for family security and family fun while our children are still living at home.

A budget can allow us to spend money without guilt. If we've budgeted to spend money on dinner out for the whole family, we can go out and not give it a second thought. If we've budgeted for a family vacation, we don't need to second-guess the wisdom of a trip. We can go with the assurance that the money has been appropriated for this purpose and that the family togetherness is well worth the expense.

It doesn't always take a lot of money to meet a need. I hope that by the time you finish reading this section, you will have a whole new way of looking at money, possessions, and your need of them.

15

Su Casa, Mi Casa

....

What Do We Need?

Only you can determine what your family truly needs in housing. Just remember those all-important priorities. If you buy a big new house in the most expensive part of town and your income is modest (assuming the bank would grant you a loan under such circumstances), you are going to have less income left for family fun.

Could you live in a simpler house with a lower monthly payment? Do you really need a house right now? Could you live in an apartment permanently? If not, could you live in an apartment for a while and save toward a bigger down payment?

A bigger down payment means lower monthly payments. Some economists encourage us to make small down payments and use the bank's money as long as possible. Yet that larger monthly payment haunts you for the next thirty years. Your investment may grow rapidly over those thirty years, but your children will also grow rapidly during that time. By the time the big monthly payments end and the house is yours, it will probably be too big for you because your children will have grown and gone. If the house payment is always a stretch for your pocketbook, you probably will have little left for recreation during the next thirty years. On the other hand, a small monthly payment means more cash for fun.

Closely tied to the question of what we need is the question of what we want. The answer to this question depends on your family's lifestyle. Your lifestyle will determine the size, style, and location of the house you will want to buy.

It's not enough to know exactly what we need and want; we must also be able to pay for the house of our dreams. After some young couples consider their wants and needs and then look at their finances, owning a house they want seems positively out of sight. They realize they can't have everything they want and must settle for getting the most they can for the money they have. We Americans are a resourceful people, and somehow most of us eventually find a way to finance our dreams.

Other Kinds of Housing

There are a number of other kinds of housing that may be more affordable than a single-family dwelling. Co-op apartments or condominiums are one alternative to owning a single-family home. All kinds of people are moving into these units—singles, the aging, empty nesters, and full families. This type of housing is ideal for people who want to own their own home but don't want the responsibility of a lot of maintenance work. When you buy into a co-op situation, you buy into a corporation that owns and runs the building. In addition to your monthly mortgage payment, you will pay a maintenance fee for care of the grounds and the exterior of the building.

When you own your own condominium, townhouse, or other kind of co-op apartment, you can paint, paper, and pound nails to your heart's content. The inside belongs to you.

As in most cases, this kind of housing has its advantages and disadvantages. The advantages have been stated. The disadvantages are that you will most likely have at least one common wall with your neighbors. You may hear some noise from them. You need to decide if that is a problem for you.

Probably the biggest drawback to buying a condominium or other multiple dwelling is the resale value. They do not escalate in value as much as single-family dwellings and may be more difficult to sell.

Another drawback can be the financial health of the developer. Check to see that he or she is highly reputable, well financed, and experienced in the field. This is especially true of a new development.

The most affordable private housing is a mobile home. When you buy a mobile home, you get the complete package, and once set up, it is ready to be lived in.

There are fees to park the home in a mobile home park. There are also installation fees, and some mobile parks specify that the homes must be set on concrete and have skirting and steps to the door. There will be plumbing and electrical hookup fees, as well.

Insurance for a mobile home is higher than for a comparably sized conventional house. Mobile homes often fall victim to fires and wind damage, and this has caused insurance rates to skyrocket.

The greatest disadvantage to mobile homes is that instead of increasing in value like a conventional single-family dwelling, they tend to depreciate, like a car. Mobile homes may provide a quick remedy to a housing need, but one needs to think seriously about the loss of investment earnings with such a home. The other obvious problem with a mobile home is the lack of space and storage, both of which are in short supply.

Weigh the needs of your family and decide the best housing for your situation.

Some people buy a piece of land and then install a used mobile home that has already taken the serious depreciation that happens in the first five years. This can give them an opportunity to begin living on their own land as they begin construction of a conventional home.

Only you can weigh the needs of your family and decide what is best in your situation. Perhaps mobile home living will give you the needed funds for family vacations and fun times. Perhaps living in a mobile home and building your permanent dream house together as a family would be a great way to build strength into your family life.

Look at your house as a wonderful place to rear your family, a possession in which you can take pride, and a great investment. In most places in the country, real estate still steadily increases in value.

The Decorating Shoestring

After a house is purchased, there's a lot more to do to make it a home. A home means furnishings, appliances, entertainment equipment, rugs, curtains, pictures, dishes, pots and pans, ad infinitum. Several years ago I met a group of women from Titusville, Florida, who really opened my eyes to the possibilities of decorating economically.

Free your mind to create new things from old.

These women formed a team to help other women decorate their houses. Sometimes they helped a young woman who didn't have much money or much imagination; sometimes it was an older person who just couldn't do the painting and sewing anymore; and sometimes it was someone who just needed some new ideas. These women think of their efforts as a ministry. They charge nothing for their help.

Their plan of action is to come to a home and look it over carefully. They assess what they can use as it is; what can be moved to another room to work better; and what paint, wallpaper, and fabrics can do to make the house a more pleasing place to be. Then, on the appointed day, they come back in force—tools, paintbrushes, and sewing machines in hand—and in eight to twelve hours they transform the whole place. They sew, paint, wallpaper, clean carpets, move furniture, and make and hang draperies. They perform miracles, using an abundance of fabric to accomplish their miracles, often sheets or sheeting fabric. Titusville has a sheet fabric outlet store, and these women are probably the store's best customers.

They don't believe any piece of furniture has to stay in the room for which it was purchased. If a corner cupboard works better in the bedroom than in the dining room, they may just move it there. These women gave me the courage to move a dresser, which had been purchased for use in the bedroom, into the dining room for use as storage for table linens. That particular house had lots of built-in storage in the bedroom, and there was no use for the chest there. It worked very well in the dining room. In the next house it was needed in the bedroom again.

All kinds of wonderful things can be done inexpensively if we can free up our thinking and begin to look at everything in a new way.

Free your mind to create new things from old things. Old pieces of oriental carpet can be made into throw pillows; colorful quilts can be hung on walls to cover plaster damage; old boots and shoes can be turned into planters for a patio; lace tablecloths can be hung for curtains; clever T-shirts with the openings sewn shut can be turned into pillows for kids' beds; wonderful old teapots with missing lids can be stuffed with dried flowers to make beautiful arrangements. There is no end to what can be done. The clue is to begin to see things in a different way than you have in the past. Don't limit your mind to what has always been.[7]

As soon as the front door of your home is opened, visitors will immediately know a lot about you, your family, and your lifestyle. How your home is furnished will indicate what is important in your life. Let me say here that there is no right or wrong way to furnish a home or to live. It is important that you find a style that is comfortable and right for your family and your situation. Children who are reared in a home where they are not allowed to sit on the furniture or touch anything are probably going to grow up to become either rigid and fussy about things or they are going to completely rebel and become sloppy and careless about possessions.[8]

Buying Furniture

So what are the basic furnishings your family needs? First of all, remember that furniture is one of the biggest investments you will make in your lifetime. You will live with whatever you choose for a long time.

Few couples just starting out can afford to buy a whole houseful of furniture at one time but they can put together a five- or ten-year plan and begin carefully buying a few pieces at a time.

My experience has been that when I have had to wait and save for a particular piece of furniture, there is great satisfaction and joy when I am finally able to buy it.

Think about pieces that you can buy now and use in one capacity or location that could later be used in another way or moved to another part of the house. Could you buy an area rug to use in your family room now and later move to a bedroom? I did that. I bought a large remnant rug and had it bound for the recreation room. Later, when we moved into another house, I had it cut down and rebound for the office. The scraps were bound as hall runners.

If you are thinking about moving furniture or rugs from one area of the house to another, you need to coordinate color and style. Then the bright blue rug you've purchased for the family room will also work under the dining room table, in a child's room, or in a large hallway. A French Provincial cabinet can move from the bedroom to a hallway, to a teenager's bedroom. I have an antique hutch that has been used as a bookcase, a display cabinet for dishes, and a place to store office supplies. It could also be used in a bedroom to store sweaters and other clothing or in a hallway for linen storage.

If you lack ideas about how to make furniture do double duty, watch home-decorating magazines or take a tour of homes in your area. Interior decorators are not afraid to put furniture to multiple uses.

When you are ready to make your first purchases, you should have thought your plan through thoroughly. You should have decided by that time what type and size furniture will look and work best for your family. Then purchase the most essential pieces first. Probably the most essential piece of furniture is a bed. Start with a good mattress. (You spend a lot of the years of your life in bed.) You can put the mattress on the floor until you can afford a bed. Next buy a couch, table, chairs, a couple of good reading lamps, a dresser or chest of some kind, and a full-length mirror.

It is amazing what people will throw out or give away. You will probably be able to fill out your basic needs with purchases

> It is amazing what people will throw out or give away.

made at garage sales, thrift shops, secondhand stores, through classified ads, and even by watching what people throw away on community cleanup days. I once read about a man in New York City who managed to put together a complete set of original Hitchcock chairs just by watching what his neighbors put out on their trash pile. That happened a long time ago, and today people seldom throw away antique furniture but they do still throw away a lot of good stuff.

Remember that well-made furniture frames can be reupholstered and solid furniture can be refinished or painted. Let me tell you about a couple of purchases I made that turned out to be winners. I bought a small upholstered armchair at the Salvation Army for fifteen dollars. Labels on the bottom of the chair indicated the chair had originally come from a manufacturer of high quality. The store label was still in place, and this told me that the chair had been purchased from a store that dealt in high-quality merchandise. The upholstery was soiled and an ugly color.

Save money on quality furniture by purchasing unfinished furniture.

My son likes to tear apart old furniture, so he pulled the upholstery off the chair. I purchased about eight yards of fabric in a lovely print that coordinated with my existing color scheme and set about slowly reupholstering the chair. Then I found a beat-up old hassock and reupholstered it as well. The result was a lovely little armchair in the exact colors I wanted, with a matching hassock. I had used a Laura Ashley chair as an inspiration. That chair sold for more than $700 with the hassock; my whole project cost $75.

Another time I found a Martha Washington armchair for six dollars. This time I got into a little more expense. Some of the rungs were missing, and I had new ones turned to match the existing rungs. Then I had the frame stripped and refinished professionally, since at that point in my life I had more money than time. Finally I had the chair reupholstered professionally. The total cost was $250, but that is a far cry from the ones I had seen in Colonial Williamsburg with a price tag of $700.

It is also possible to save money on quality furniture by purchasing unfinished furniture and furniture kits. These pieces have often been presanded. Some assembly may be required in addition to sanding and finishing. Stores and companies selling this furniture can give advice and sell you the products you will need to produce lovely furniture. If you are careful, you could end up with a piece of furniture that is better than commercially finished furniture. After all, yours will be hand-finished. It is important to work slowly and thoroughly and not ignore any of the suggested steps.

When purchasing furniture for a family, think comfort first—seating comfort and sleeping comfort. Then think about fabric. Can it be cleaned? Is the design basic enough so that the piece can be reupholstered easily and therefore less expensively?

Classically designed furniture makes good sense. Designs that have been popular for two hundred years will not go out of style next year.

Where to Find Furniture

Your local furniture store will probably have a good sale once or twice this year, but did you know that these same furniture stores often have a warehouse where they sell one-of-a-kind pieces, last year's models, closeouts, and damaged pieces? I have not bought an appliance or a piece of furniture in a regular store for years. Not only are prices cheaper at the warehouses than in the stores on an everyday basis, but the warehouses get overstocked sometimes and have sales. When that happens, prices are often cut from 50 to 70 percent.

All you have to do is go to your local furniture store and pick out what you like. Get the model numbers, fabric name, and so forth. Then look in the back of almost any decorating or home magazine and find an ad that says, "Buy furniture direct from the manufacturer." Often there is a toll-free number to call. Call and tell them what you want. They'll figure out a way to get it for you. They'll give you an exact price for the piece and tell you what the shipping charges will be. There will be no surprises.

The last time I bought furniture this way, I was required to get two cashier's checks, one for the furniture itself and the other for the freight. I had them waiting when the furniture was delivered.

Another wonderful way to get top-quality furniture at bargain prices is to watch for furniture stores going out of business. Many times I have purchased top-of-the-line furniture for the dealer's cost.

How Can I Know Excellent Quality?

Here are some guidelines for recognizing quality in furniture:

- Check the joints of drawers. They should be clean and tight fitting. Quality furniture will have dovetailed joinings.
- Drawers should slide smoothly.
- Furniture doors should be well hung and fitted.
- Backs and undersides of furniture should be of wood and should be finished.
- Check the finish. It should be smooth and of an even application.
- Check the hardware. Is it appropriate to the piece? Is it the same quality as the piece? Is it firmly attached?
- For upholstered furniture, ask to see literature or a model that shows how the interior of the piece is made. Stuffing can cover a massive amount of poor workmanship.
- Buy well-known brand names from reputable stores. If the prices seem too high, save and wait for the really big sales.
- Most upholstered furniture does not have a warranty. The exception is mattresses, which are usually guaranteed by the manufacturer for ten to twenty years.

Floor Coverings

There are lots of options in floor coverings. Once again, it is important to consider the lifestyle of your family. If you have a house full of sports enthusiasts who are tracking equipment, grass, mud, snow, or other unmentionables into the house on a regular basis, you may want to consider using a lot of easy-care, no-wax vinyl flooring.

If you love beautiful old furniture, it will show up best in a room with solid wood floors and area rugs. Wood floors come in softwood and hardwood. Pine flooring is quite soft, and while it is very beautiful, it will dent from high-heeled shoes or dropped items. It also wears down more quickly and must be refinished more often.

Hardwood floors, on the other hand, are usually white or red oak. They, too, will dent, but not as easily as softwood floors. I love hardwood floors because they are very beautiful and I find them very easy to care for. I prefer something called a Swedish finish, which requires (infrequently) a quick wipe with white vinegar and water. In between times, a quick swish around the room with a dustmop keeps them lovely.

Of course, the all-time favorite for floor covering is wall-to-wall carpet. It's a favorite for a number of reasons. One is the warmth underfoot. Another is that carpeting reduces noise. Since the advent of man-made fibers for carpeting, wall-to-wall rugs are quite easy to care for and they come in a wide range of colors, styles, and patterns—something for every income and taste.

One mark of a quality carpet is its density.

In choosing carpet, buy the best you can afford. Here is a place where it really makes sense, in the long run, to buy quality. Quality carpets have a longer life and do not need to be replaced as often; they are made of better fibers and will not take as much care; the colors will not fade with repeated cleanings or exposure to sunlight; they will not pill up, mat, or otherwise become unattractive.

One mark of a quality carpet is its density. The way to check the density of a carpet is to fold a piece of it in half, back to back. If the fibers on the surface are still thick and it is hard to see the backing, you are holding a good piece of carpet. But if, on the other hand, there is a space between tufts of fibers and the backing is all too easy to see, you are holding a poor-quality piece. Price, unfortunately, is another way to check for quality. High-quality carpeting costs more than poor-quality carpeting.

Carpeting should be installed over the best grade of padding you can afford. Padding gives a cushioned feeling underfoot, and more important, padding extends the life of the carpet.

Carpet should be purchased from a reputable dealer and should be installed by a reputable installer. This is not the place to make any major mistakes. There is too much money involved.

There is a new idea in carpet sales, called mobile service. The dealer will come to your home not only with carpet samples, but with a video camera. He takes a picture of your room and then, through the magic of computer technology, he shows you how various kinds and colors of carpeting will look on your floors. You don't have to go to a local carpet store and be overwhelmed by choices. You don't have to wonder what that color carpet will look like on your floor. You don't even have to leave the comfort of your home to see, decide, and set up all the arrangements for the installation of carpet in your home.

Appliances

I have a hard time getting excited about appliances, but that's probably not a good attitude, since they can eat up a huge hunk of a furnishing budget. We need to know what we are doing when we buy appliances.

Appliances are our friends, our helpers—the workhorses of our existence. Once again, it is important to determine what your family needs.

Here are some guidelines for buying appliances:

- Don't buy on impulse. Plan your purchases.
- Don't buy more than you need. Buy no-frills.
- Buy when the appliances are on sale.
- Shop for model closeouts, markdowns, and so forth.
- Find out if the appliance will fit where you want to put it.
- Consider whether it will be large enough for future needs as your family grows.
- Find out what the purchase price includes. Does it include delivery? set-up? warranty? service?
- Find out the average life expectancy of this appliance.

Save money on appliances by buying secondhand.

It is possible to save money on appliances by buying second-hand. Watch the newspaper classified ads for these items. People often opt to sell their appliances rather than move them, even though these items may not be old, and the sellers may take a considerable loss. Most appliances are very heavy and add significantly to the cost of moving to another part of the country.

Remember that the expected life of a washing machine is eleven years, so a washer that is only five years old could have at least six years left, and probably more. A clothes dryer is estimated to have at least a fourteen-year lifespan, although in my experience it is the dryer that wears out first.

When buying used appliances, you will be buying "as is," and there is a risk involved, but even extensive repairs will probably cost much less than the price of new machines.

Accessories

Accessory items—lamps, pictures, pillows, and so forth—are the jewels of your home. They are the little touches that give your home your style and make it unique to your family's personality.

Accessory items can be very expensive. You can literally spend a fortune on them, but it isn't necessary to do so. We are living in a time when handicrafts have made a resurgence, and it is easy to buy them in shops, at fairs, and at craft shows. It is also possible to learn how to make them yourself.

Most people collect something. I've been picking up black and white china dogs for my son for years. I collect red and white pottery. My daughter collects hats and other costume materials.

Your choice of accessory items will be limited only by your imagination.

Many children collect rocks, shells, birds' nests, and other natural items. These items can be viewed as junk or messy collections or they can be displayed in some attractive way and kept as "treasures of childhood." I have jars of various kinds of stones, shells, crystals, and beach glass we picked up over the years. I bought some inexpensive storage jars with pretty tops. The collected items look very pretty in them and make a nice accessory for a bathroom or in a window where the sun shines through the crystals and beach glass.

Your choice of accessory items will be limited only by your imagination. Each person in a family should have some input as to the decoration of a home, and each person should have some space that is just his. Children, as soon as they are old enough, should help decide on the decor and accessories of their room. They may not do their room the way you would, but it is important that they have a place to express their own taste.

For small children, put shelves low enough so they can put their accessory items (which will be stuffed animals and other toys) where they can see them. They are not going to observe much that is above their eye level. Low shelves will also encourage them to put away their toys by themselves.

The possibilities for making a shell of a house a true home are unlimited. Just pick up any home magazine in a supermarket today and your mind will be boggled by the possibilities. Create a style that is unique to your family and your way of life. Choose a style that lets your family relax and be at home. Make it a place where all your friends and their friends love to come.

The next few pages will give you lots of good, quick, money-saving ideas for home decorating.

Ideas for Saving Money on Home Decorating

Furniture

1. Watch the classified ads for items you need. These may be sold through garage sales or directly to you. Always offer less than the asking price; you may be amazed at how little you will pay.

2. Check out resale and consignment shops that sell furniture and accessory items.

3. Search out warehouses that sell one-of-a-kind or closeout models. Get on their mailing lists for sales. Watch newspapers and television for notification of sales.

4. Visit auctions. Most auctions have an inspection time ahead of the actual event. Take advantage of that time and inspect the items carefully. If you don't know how to buy at auction, go with someone who does and observe and learn before you begin bidding.

5. High-quality furniture stores have excellent sales several times a year. Learn when the item you want will be on sale.

6. Buy from furniture marts in East Coast manufacturing towns, either in person or by phone. This can be facilitated by ordering the *Wholesale-by-Mail Catalog* (Lowell Miller and Prudence McCullough, St. Martins, 1994).

7. Shop unfinished-furniture stores for high-quality furniture at a reasonable price. Sometimes you can buy finished display pieces for less than in a regular furniture store.

8. If you cannot afford the latest in upholstered furniture, get good used furniture and slipcover or reupholster it in the fabric of your choice. Pattern companies have very simple patterns for slipcovers. Often there are classes available for learning how to do reupholstery.

9. If the upholstery of a used piece is in good condition and you can live with the color, add lots of accessory items—pillows, matching table skirts, valances, and so forth.

10. Make a full-length cloth for a round table. You can put anything with a round top under such a table skirt. It is possible to purchase pressboard rounds with legs that screw on at fabric stores and through mail order catalogs. Mine is a round of plywood screwed to an old nightstand.

11. Paint furniture if the finish can no longer be restored. Stencil designs on the painted furniture for a fresh country look.

12. Watch for ideas for building simple furniture for the family room and other casual areas of your home. It is fairly simple to build a banquette by building a low box with a platform

top and then adding a single mattress, bolsters, oversized pillows for the top. Add an upholstery slipcover to the mattress.

13. Investigate a simple slipcover treatment for outdoor wire chairs, folding wooden chairs, and so forth. By adding a simple slipcover, you can transform these utilitarian items into lovely indoor decorator items. Some of the slipcovers have big bows in the back, which make them charming for a bedroom or a little girl's room.

Accessories

14. Make country throw pillows from plaid dish towels or cotton kerchiefs.

15. Glue four six-inch tiles together at the corners with tacky glue to make a lovely cachepot.

Paint and Paper

16. Paint stools in bright colors for the kitchen.

17. Experiment with sponge-painting techniques. You can obtain some interesting results on furniture, walls, and ceilings.

18. Paint terra-cotta pots in matching colors. The paint makes them less porous and they will hold moisture better. Prime them before painting.

19. Paint galvanized buckets for the kids' rooms. Add decals or paint on fun pictures.

20. Cover an old footlocker or trunk with gift wrap or maps. Add a dozen coats of shellac for a rock-hard finish that will last for years.

21. Watch for patterns, stencils, and ideas in magazines for painting furniture and adding decorative borders to walls.

22. Investigate the lovely finishes that can be achieved through color washes.

23. If you can't afford a carpet or rug for your bare floor, paint a design on it. That's what early settlers did. Use a checkerboard pattern or stencil a design directly on the floor.

24. Use decoupage to disguise damaged furniture finishes.

25. Paint a checkerboard cloth design on an outdoor picnic table.

Miscellaneous

26. Check out the pattern books in fabric stores for patterns for valances, curtains, pillows, and a multitude of other decorator items.

27. Think about ways to use your doors and walls for storage space. The backs of doors can be used to store magazines simply by adding a rack.

28. Use sheets and pillow ticking for decorative fabrics. Use lots of these fabrics for a luxurious look.

29. Use a section of picket fence in the opening of a fireplace. Bank it with potted plants or real or artificial greenery for a fresh summer look.

30. Cover damaged walls with fabric. Some use a light padding behind the fabric for a luxurious look. Seams can be covered by gluing braid over them or by adding simple wooden trim painted a matching color.

31. Pad and upholster a headboard of a bed to coordinate with the bedspread and other fabrics used in the room.

Decorating for Christmas

32. Use cookie cutters as ornaments for the tree or hang them on a cord strung across a window. Cookie cutters come in bright colors, copper, or silver.

33. A big wooden bowl of cookie cutters with a few shiny balls tossed in makes a nice decoration for a kitchen or family room.

34. Have your children make paper snowflakes. Tape them to a window and spray artificial snow through them to transfer the pattern to the window.

35. Heap a wooden garden tool carrier with pinecones. Tie a bright plaid bow to the handle. Put it in a hallway.

36. Use the same wooden tool carrier without the pinecones as a place to put Christmas cards. Keep it in the living room or the family room where everyone can enjoy the cards.

37. Spray paint pinecones in white and gold and pile in a gilt basket for a table decoration.

38. Spray paint bay leaves a golden color and add them to a bowl of potpourri for a festive look.

39. Thread shiny balls onto velvet ribbons, wire on pinecones, and use them to tie back drapes.

40. Hang a tiny birdhouse on the wall of a room. Add some greenery and a plaid bow.

41. Stalks of wheat tied with a bright red velvet bow makes a nice decoration for the outside of a house and a great gift for the birds.

42. If your children like to collect birds' nests, use them for decoration. Some can be set on the branches of the Christmas tree. Others grouped together will make a lovely buffet display when mixed with greens, red berries, and tiny bows. Fill the nest with wooden eggs.

43. Use cut greens as bouquets. Put them in interesting bottles, pots, brass or copper buckets, or just about anything you have that will hold water. Cut evergreens kept in water will last throughout the holidays. The greens can be sprayed lightly with glue and brushed with glitter that looks like frost crystals. Add a red velvet bow.

44. Wreaths and swags can be made from almost any imaginable substance. Of course evergreen and holly wreaths are traditional and very nice, if you can cut the greens yourself. But you can also wire brightly wrapped Christmas candy to a styrofoam ring. Use old-fashioned hairpins to do this. Attach a tiny pair of children's scissors to the wreath with a ribbon for cutting loose the pieces of candy.

45. Use pasta in bow tie and wheel shapes to make a kitchen wreath. Glue the pasta as close together as possible on the styrofoam base.

46. If you live where you can buy them reasonably, use hot peppers wired together to form a Southwestern wreath.

47. Wire bay leaves together to form a fragrant wreath.

48. Poke loops of ribbons that have been wired at the bottom into a styrofoam base as close together as possible to completely hide the base. You can also attach the loops of ribbons with pins.

49. Make a wreath using loops of cornhusks. You may need to soften them in water to bend them into loops. Mix the cornhusk loops with calico ribbon loops.

50. Form a wreath of baby's breath and greens. Encircle it with lots of tiny lights.

51. Use collectibles such as seashells for a wreath. Glue them to a styrofoam base or add to greens.

52. At the end of the Christmas season, watch for Christmas china. It doesn't have to be expensive, and after the holidays, it should be available for half-price. It will make your holiday table special.

53. A centerpiece can be a bowl of red and green apples. Tuck in stick cinnamon tied with tiny red plaid bows.

54. Use the children's teddy bears for a corner display. Tie Christmas bows around their necks. It doesn't matter if the bears are worn.

55. Let the children string cranberries and wind them with greens to make a garland for doors, windows, or a lamppost.

56. Use a child's sled for a fireside or doorside decoration. Add some greens and a bow or two. Even an old snow shovel can be turned into an outdoor Christmas decoration by adding a big plaid bow and a bunch of greens. Put it right by the front door.

57. Make simple Christmas stockings from elegant tapestry remnants—or use velvet, lamé, or other luxurious fabrics. Add lots of metallic trim, sequins, or embroidery in gold thread.

58. Remember that food is beautiful. Display Christmas goodies in clear glass jars and other storage containers.

16

Put Another Potato in the Soup

When we were children, we used to groan when Mom made a huge turkey or an extra-large casserole dish. We knew we'd end up eating it all—either now or later. That's how she stretched her meager food budget.

Every year that passes, it takes more money to put food on the family table. The bottom line of making food dollars stretch is having an attitude that says:

I'm going to make do with less expensive products.

I'm going to honor my own wants and not be controlled by advertising.

I'm going to buy food value over food convenience whenever possible.

I'm going to learn how to cook less expensive cuts of meat in a way that makes them taste as good as the more expensive cuts. And I'm going to use less meat in family meals.

I'm going to plan my menus before I go to the store to help me avoid impulse buying.

I'm going to see if the nonfood items I buy at the grocery store could be purchased more cheaply at another place.

There are many factors that affect how much you must spend on food for your family. Some of them are:

the amount of available income

the age of your family members (teenagers have hollow arms and legs that need hourly filling)

how much and what kind of entertaining you do

the kinds of foods you prefer

where you live

weather conditions

whether you grow or process any of your own food

how much you eat out

how important food is to you, as compared to other wants and needs

inflation

family traditions surrounding food and eating

Food is the biggest item in every family's weekly budget, and there is no way you can get by without eating. You have to find a way to eat more economically without jeopardizing nutrition or seriously lowering your quality of life. The challenge is to find a way to cut down your food costs without anyone in the family realizing you're saving money on food.

Vegetarian cookbooks are good sources for how to season with herbs.

You can slash your costs more than 20 percent merely by "trading down" to products that are just as nutritious as expensive "convenience" items. The question always comes down to: Do you have more time or money? If you have more money than time, buy convenience; if you have more time than money, trade down to less expensive, less convenient products.

To stretch our family's food dollar, I figured out ways to use every bit of leftover food and disguise it so that no one knew it was making an encore. I kept a stockpot in the refrigerator, where little bits and pieces of leftovers were tossed, along with water from cooking vegetables and meat juices. Then I would add some fresh vegetables and lots of herbs and make soup for Saturday night suppers. Each week the soup had a slightly different texture and flavor, but it was always delicious. Served with homemade corn bread or baking powder biscuits hot from the oven, supper didn't taste like leftovers.

My friend Candy is a master at making money stretch, and her food dollars are no exception. I love to stop by her apartment, because it always smells so good. There is usually something wonderful simmering in a pot. I've eaten some of her cooking, and it tastes just as good as it smells. I asked her for her secrets.

Candy decided to invest her limited funds in some herbs and try her hand at ethnic cooking. She bought the herbs a few packets at a time at an import store, where they are much less expensive than the fancy bottled kind that supermarkets sell.

Then she acquired a few good ethnic cookbooks and started trying things. She tells me that vegetarian recipes are the best, and that it is simple to add some kind of meat to a vegetarian recipe if you are not a vegetarian. The vegetarian cookbooks have the best information for seasoning foods with herbs.

Then she takes simple cuts of beef, pork, lamb, or poultry and spices them up. Cheaper, tougher cuts of meat can be marinated to tenderize them. Various kinds of cheese and other dairy products can provide needed protein in the diet.

She doesn't use much prepared food because it is always higher in price and she also uses lots of whole grains in her cooking. Grains such as rice, bulgur, wheat, and corn all add substantial nutrition at an inexpensive price.

Candy says, "Use artistry in the kitchen. Cooking can satisfy a creative urge as much as songwriting or painting." She also encourages low-fat cooking. "Sometimes instead of buying some fattening food, I buy a bunch of fresh flowers to keep me from feeling deprived. One bunch of mixed flowers will make several little color-spot bouquets."

Free Food

If you don't have a lot of money for food, you have to use your head and think about how to make your food dollars stretch. It is amazing to me how much food is wasted in this country. In many parts of the country, wild berry vines droop with unpicked fruit.

Last summer I walked two blocks from the house with a couple of buckets and returned in about half an hour with enough blackberries to make twelve pints of jelly. In most areas of the country, there are all kinds of wild berries to be picked.

Everywhere there are abandoned fruit trees from which you can glean apples, plums, pears, and other kinds of fruit. You do have to trim the fruit, watching for worms and other pests, but some people pay high prices for fruit grown without insecticides. Be sure to check with the owner of private property before picking berries or fruit.

There's probably some free food in your area. I remember a time in California when a major packing plant went on strike at the height of the pear harvest. We drove out to the plant to discover mountains of pears slowly turning into a brown mass that smelled like vinegar. Since we had been away when the strike began, we were not as fortunate as our friends who brought home boxes and boxes of perfect fruit that they canned for winter.

Gathering free food is time-consuming. As far as I am concerned, there is nothing more tedious than picking huckleberries. I couldn't be persuaded to do it if it wasn't so wonderful to sit in the sunshine on a hillside and talk with others who are also picking. It's a kind of therapy that money cannot buy.

Food Warehouses

Food warehouses sell canned goods at a discount because the label isn't right, there has been a slight overcook on the processing, something has been spilled on the canned goods and made a mess of the labels, or the case has been broken.

Manufacturers don't have the time or money to replace labels or repackage broken cases, so all the damaged goods are purchased by food warehouses and resold at greatly reduced prices.

It is important to inspect cans for damage, just as it is important to inspect cans in a regular food store. Don't buy cans with rusted tops or bulging sides. Report them to the store's owner.

If you have a question about the quality of a certain brand of food, you can always buy one can and take it home and try it before buying more. Or you can carry a can opener with you, purchase one can, take it outside, open it, and inspect or taste it for quality. If it passes, go back inside and stock up.

There's a milling company in the Seattle area that sells whole-grain products. Most of the milling is done on-site, so it's a dusty place. The milled grains are stored in large rubber garbage cans. You have to scoop and package your own grain products.

The store sells everything from steel-cut oatmeal to millet. They also have whole, unroasted, unsalted nuts, a full line of herbs, cornmeal and all kinds of flour, bulk raisins and other dried fruit, lentils, beans, and dried peas. They carry coffee in bulk, as well as carob and chocolate chips. Here is a place where your money buys so much that you can barely stagger out under the weight of twenty dollars worth of food.

Food ware-houses have some excellent products and bargains.

I have also visited mills where grain is still being ground on old-fashioned millstones powered by water. Visiting such a place with your family will help them understand how early settlers managed to take care of one aspect of their food needs.

Other kinds of food warehouses have sprung up in recent years—giant food warehouses where you can buy in bulk. Usually there is a membership fee, and you must weigh the cost of the membership fee, the ability to buy only in bulk (which can sometimes present storage problems), the wide variety of food that simply begs to be purchased, and the actual savings. Most warehouses will give you a trial shopping trip before you purchase a membership.

I find that although the savings are substantial, when I'm shopping at such warehouses, I spend more than I had intended and then have to find a place to store the food. However, if time is a factor, it will be timesaving to buy in bulk. I have discovered some excellent products and bargains at these warehouses.

For example, one such warehouse sells frozen boneless, skinless chicken breasts, which have virtually become a staple at our house. They are low in cholesterol, easily stored in the freezer, and quickly cooked by thawing in the microwave. Then they can be fully cooked in the microwave in three minutes, or broiled or pan-fried in olive oil and seasonings in just minutes. I have also discovered that this warehouse's ground beef is extra lean and of excellent quality. It comes, however, only in fifteen-pound packages.

Growing Your Own

Not only can growing your own food save you money, but it can provide you with fresh, nutritious, tasty meals. While I was growing up, my dad's garden provided much of what our family ate. Dad still has a garden that is so beautiful people stop and lean over the fence to look at weedless rows of beans, peas, corn, chard, asparagus, potatoes, beets, carrots, raspberries, cabbage, and kohlrabies.

If you enjoy gardening, and if you are willing to process the foods you grow, then growing your own food can be an excellent way to save money. There are many ways to process foods for long-term storage. Depending on the product and the equipment you have available, you may want to can, dehydrate, or freeze what you grow. Be sure to follow directions for the method you choose so that you end up with safe and nutritious food. Products that have been improperly canned may be lethal.

A home freezer is a good moneysaving investment.

If you have a dehydrating unit, you can take advantage of supermarket sales of overripe fruit. Fruit has the most sugar when it is fully ripe, but it will not survive long on the store's shelves, so you can often find bananas for a few cents a pound and peaches and pears at the peak of ripeness.

These fruits are wonderful when sliced and dehydrated. They make great nutritious snacks, and the homemade variety is superior to the kind you can buy in health-food stores. Most fruit snacks in health-food stores have been treated to keep them from turning brown.

You may also want to dry green peppers and mushrooms when they are inexpensive. Toss them in to soups or casseroles. Herbs that you grow or buy can also be dried.

Freezing is probably the easiest way to preserve food. Owning a home freezer may be one of the best moneysaving investments you can make.

When you own a freezer, not only can you freeze fruits and vegetables at the peak of their season, but you can stock up on breads, pies, cakes, and cookies from a bakery thrift store. You can also buy a side of beef or a lot of chicken when the price drops, or just take advantage of meat specials at the supermarket each week.

Ideas for Saving Food Dollars

1. Always use a shopping list. Buy only what you need, but be sure to buy everything you need for a particular dish. That way you will not have to go back for more ingredients. Every trip to the supermarket causes you to spend added food dollars. How many times have you gone for one item and come out with a bagful of food?

2. Buy eggs. If your cholesterol level can stand it, eggs are a good source of protein and are usually cheap.

3. Buy the least expensive kind of cheddar cheese for cooking. Buy a better cheese for snacking.

4. Use skim milk for cooking. It's better for you and cheaper than reconstituted dry milk.

5. Shop without the kids. They can sabotage your food budget.

6. Don't shop when you are tired or hungry or when the store is crowded because you won't be able to think through your purchases.

7. Use coupons, but be careful not to buy more expensive items just because you have a coupon. Think it through before buying.

8. Buy generic or store brands. If you have a question as to their quality, buy one and try it. If it meets your standard, stock up on the next trip.

9. Buy "raw" food whenever possible. Remember that every time someone does something to your food, it adds to the cost. Besides that, you don't know what they have added

to your food. Prepackaged, precooked, prebreaded, pre-anything adds dollars to your food bill.

10. Pancakes made from a dry mix are cheaper than frozen pancakes and cheaper than a ready-pour mix.

11. Buy seasonal fruits and vegetables. Not only are they less expensive, they also taste better when they are at the peak of the season. Melons picked in midsummer always taste better than the first ones that appear in supermarkets in the spring.

12. When fruits and vegetables are at their peak, think about freezing some for use later on. Broccoli is very cheap at certain times of year. All you need to do is wash it thoroughly, blanch it in hot water for a couple of minutes, cool it under cold running water, and package it for the freezer.

13. Remember that extra packaging raises prices. Buy huge bags of potato chips and repackage in smaller plastic bags. (They freeze well.) Buy a large container of instant oatmeal, rather than the small packets.

14. Buy cheese in bulk and spend a few minutes shredding it for topping casseroles and other dishes. Package in the amount needed for one dish. Cheese can be frozen if used for cooking.

15. Buy potatoes, carrots, onions, and grapefruit in large sacks. They are considerably cheaper than the individual items.

16. Grind your own coffee at the store and save, but stay away from gourmet coffee beans if you want to save money.

17. Buy raisins in two-pound bags and repackage for snacks.

18. Sugared cereals are more expensive by far. Buy the unsugared variety and sweeten it at home.

19. If possible, teach your kids to eat whole grain cereals such as oatmeal and other cooked grains. They are more nutritious and less expensive.

20. Mix your own salad dressings from packaged mixes. You'll save significantly over bottled dressings.

21. Vegetables frozen in butter and those with other added seasonings and ingredients are nearly twice the price of

the plain ones. By adding your own butter and herbs, you can save big.

22. Nothing could be easier to make than the new muffin mixes, and they are cheap. Buy them instead of fresh muffins from the bakery counter.

23. Use up leftover meat and poultry by grinding it with onions, a dash of Worcestershire, mustard, and mayonnaise for a hearty sandwich spread.

24. Sliver pork, chicken, or beef leftovers and stir-fry with fresh vegetables.

25. Crumble meat loaf and add it to spaghetti sauce.

26. Bits and pieces of ham or turkey can be added to an ordinary salad to turn it into a great chef's salad.

27. Sliver cold leftover roast beef and serve it with a side dish. Hot Chinese mustard and sesame seeds make it special.

28. Add cooked leftover vegetables to omelets.

29. Mash up the inside of leftover baked potatoes with a little milk until fluffy. Pile the potato back into the skin, top with cheese, bacon bits, onions, and reheat in the microwave.

30. Cook sliced onion in butter or margarine until just tender. Then add sliced leftover potatoes. Heat through. Add shredded cheese, put a lid on the pan, and remove it from the heat. In a few minutes the cheese will be melted into the potatoes.

31. Serve leftover spaghetti cold as an oriental salad. Use a little soy sauce for seasoning, and add some sesame seeds.

32. Make croutons from dry bread.

33. Turn dry bread into crumbs by chopping it in the blender. These are great browned in butter and sprinkled over vegetables.

34. Make an elegant English trifle using leftover cake—preferably pound cake or angel food. Layer cake with peaches or raspberries, custard pudding, whipped cream, and toasted almonds.

35. Eat popcorn instead of chips. It's much cheaper and better for you.

36. Teach your kids to make cinnamon toast instead of filling up on cupcakes and other filled pastries.

37. Learn to eat simple desserts such as fruit and cookies, puddings, and frozen yogurt, rather than more expensive pies and cakes.

38. Use old-fashioned rice that has to be cooked twenty minutes, rather than instant rice that takes five minutes and costs twice as much. You can probably afford the extra fifteen minutes.

39. Check different forms of food—fresh, frozen, canned—to see which is the best buy. Do not assume one form is always cheaper than another.

40. Limit purchases of perishable foods, even when they are a great bargain. You are not saving money if the excess has to be thrown out.

41. Buy food in large containers if your family can consume it before it spoils. It is usually considerably cheaper (and more environmentally sound) than several small containers. Compare prices.

42. Select cuts and types of meat, poultry, and fish that provide the most cooked lean meat for the money spent. Some of the less expensive cuts can also be the most flavorful but must be prepared properly to tenderize them.

43. When buying a turkey, pick a large one. You get more meat per pound on a bird weighing twelve or more pounds.

44. Buy boneless meat cuts whenever possible. Pound for pound, they're cheaper.

45. Serve less meat and mix it with vegetables, pastas, rice, and breads to make a little go farther.

46. Remove the fat from meat drippings and use the rest of the juices to flavor gravies, soups, and sauces.

47. Prepare meatless meals a couple times a week. Use beans, dry peas, and peanut butter as a protein source on those days.

17

Vogue, GQ, and Other Expensive Myths

I've always considered it a challenge to look as great as I can and spend as little money as possible. It's a game for me, and I've become quite skilled at it.

A standard line I hear from my friends is, "That's a beautiful outfit. Where did you get it?" When I smile slyly, they say, "Don't tell me how little you paid. I don't want to hear."

One day a friend and I were discussing an outfit I was wearing that happened to be made up of bits and pieces I had picked up over a number of years in a number of places. Finally she threw her head back and laughed. "You look like you stepped out of the pages of *Vogue* magazine, and when I add you up, you total about ten dollars. How do you do it?"

Well, I'm not going to tell all my secrets here, but I am going to share some of the principles I've learned to make clothing dollars stretch for every member of the family.

Buy Quality

If you buy a marvelous trendy suit for a very inexpensive price, but it starts to bag where you sit and the seams split out after you've worn it only a couple of times, you haven't really bought a bargain. By the time you replace your bargain garment, you may have spent more than if you'd bought a more expensive, better quality suit in the first place.

Think in terms of investing in clothing. If you buy a three-hundred-dollar suit and wear it five years, that's only sixty dollars a year. It's possible to wear a classically styled, well-made garment even longer.

But there is a problem. With so many clothing options available, how do you find quality products? What is quality, anyway? There are some things you can look for. Here are some tips to help you determine top-caliber clothing.

* Check the tag for fiber content. Natural fibers are always winners in the quality category, because they breathe. One-hundred-percent woolen garments can't be beaten for wearability, packability, and holding their shape, especially if they are lined. One-hundred-percent-cotton garments need a lot of care to keep them looking their best (they wrinkle) but they *are* comfortable.

* Sewn into the garment somewhere you will find a care label. Look for it and determine if this garment is going to spend more time at the cleaner's than it does in your closet. Since we are talking about saving money for family fun, think twice about purchasing a garment that requires expensive dry cleaning.

* There are all kinds of synthetic-blend fabrics. All have the advantage of easy care, but each has its own set of disadvantages as well. One synthetic fabric that is very popular right now is rayon. Rayon gives colors a brightness and intensity that is delightful. It's inexpensive, but it must be dry cleaned and it wrinkles.

* Check seam allowances. Skimpy seam allowances or those that are frayed or puckered are the mark of inferior construction. Clothing with these problems will not last long in the washer and dryer and will never look right.

✳ On permanently pressed clothing, seams, hems, and the creases are also permanently pressed. You won't be able to let out a seam or lower a hemline on these garments without a fold line showing. You can, of course, take in a seam or shorten a hem.

✳ Check the zipper. It should lie flat. There should be no puckers around it. The teeth of the zipper should be painted to match the zipper tape. The weight of the zipper should be right for the type of fabric. If too lightweight, a zipper will break quickly.

✳ Check the hem. Has a good quality hem tape been used? If it is loosely woven, it will come apart after a few washings or cleanings. Hems should have a deep allowance.

✳ Check the lining. Is it of a good quality and color to match the exterior of the garment? Is it skimpy? Is it firmly attached to the garment in such a way that it doesn't hang down at the cuff or the bottom of the garment? Well-made dresses and pants are usually lined. A lining makes the garment hang better, increases durability, and decreases wrinkling and bagging.

✳ Check the buttons. Perhaps nothing gives away the quality of a garment as quickly as its buttons. Buttons are the jewelry of the garment. Better quality garments have beautiful buttons, and manufacturers usually provide one or two extra buttons in case you lose one. Good buttons are expensive, especially if you have to replace an entire set, so look for the extras and keep them handy.

✳ Check the buttonholes. Bound buttonholes used to be the mark of quality clothing but are seldom seen anymore, even on the finest of clothing. The machine work on machine-made buttonholes should be tight and even, and there should be no threads hanging loose. Thread color should match the garment's color.

✳ Check lapels. Lapels should be crisp and rolled slightly to the underside in a quality garment. If the lapel is limp when you first see it, don't buy the garment. Limpness happens quickly enough after you take the garment home. Also check to see if the upper lapel fabric is bonded to an interfacing. Sometimes these begin to separate in a bubbly pattern after one or two washings.

✳ Check underarm seams. Do they meet exactly? In mass-produced garments, the sleeves are sewn in before the side seams are closed, and sometimes the seams do not match. While this may not matter much to the look of the finished garment, it is an indication of shoddy workmanship.

✳ Check all other seams. Puckered seams tell you the thread tension of one or both threads was set wrong and is an indication of haste. Sometimes material may be caught in the stitches, causing puckering. At other times, the garment has been improperly pressed during construction and darts and pleats are lying the wrong way for a smooth fit.

✳ Check belt eyelets. Are they smooth and finished so they won't tear out after one or two wearings? Is the belt washable on a washable garment? Is it dry cleanable on a dry cleanable garment?

✳ Check pattern match. Plaids, stripes, tattersalls, and windowpane checked patterns should all match. Check where the sleeve and jacket are joined. Plaids and patterns should meet here, as well. Misaligned patterns shout sloppy sewing.

Sewing to Have More Clothes

Home sewing can be very exciting and rewarding. There are beautiful fabrics from which to choose, designer patterns, gorgeous trim, and buttons. Knits are easy to sew, functional, and inexpensive. Serger sewing machines make the sewing of knits a snap.

If you have the time, you can sew almost any garment for yourself or your family and have it come out better than store-bought clothing. Sewing, however, is time-consuming, and you will have to determine if you are truly saving all that much by doing it.

It is wise to learn how to sew simple things, like a skirt. Well-made skirts can cost up to $125; you may be able to make the same skirt out of the same fabric for around $25. Children prefer simple clothing without a lot of fussy ruffles and trim. These can be easily constructed by the home sewer. If you can learn to make simple T-shirts for your children (a thirty-minute job), you can save a bundle, particularly if you watch for remnant pieces of fabric.

Fabric stores almost always offer instruction in making garments for both adults and children, accessory items, home decor projects, and crafts. The classes are usually free or are offered at a minimal fee. Often instructors give out coupons redeemable in fabrics and supplies. It's a great bargain.

Mending to Have More Clothes

My mother used to tell me repeatedly that if I would mend my clothes, I would have a lot more to wear. As a teenager that wasn't something I wanted to hear, but once in a while I would take her advice and mend ripped seams, sew up hems that had come loose, and sew on buttons and trim. She was right. When I mended, I did have more to wear and I also had less frustration because when I wanted to wear something, it was ready.

You can fix clothing even if you don't know how to sew. Hems, facings, interfacings, trims, and appliqués all come as iron-on fusibles. There's a stick-and-sew zipper that will still require sewing, but at least it doesn't require pins and basting. The coated tape can be stuck and restuck to fabric without spotting the fabric. There are button replacement devices that don't require a needle.

Simple fix-its such as changing buttons, re-embroidering buttonholes to get rid of frayed edges, repairing torn belt loops, replacing seam and hem tapes, and repairing puckered seams all quickly upgrade a garment.

If even these simple tasks seem overwhelming, find a seamstress to help. A good seamstress should be able to repair a large number of garments in a couple of hours, as most repairs are minor. Repairing three-corner tears and replacing frayed collars and cuffs are not easy, but still may be worth the cost if the garment is of high quality. Quality clothing is worth the time and money it takes to keep it in good repair. In the long run, you'll be saving money.

Restyling

One of the ways to extend your family's wardrobe is to remodel or restyle well-made clothing. This isn't as difficult as it may sound. Here are some ways to restyle clothing:

- Take the skirt or the jacket of a suit and pair it with lots of other tops and pants.
- Use fusible materials to help with hemming, holding a facing in place, or attaching trim to a garment.
- Take in or let out garments (unless they're permanent press) to get the best fit.
- Men's pants can usually be altered an inch or so larger or smaller.
- Cut off children's jeans and pants for summer. You don't even need to hem them, as kids prefer them ragged.
- Girls can use big brother's outgrown colored T-shirts for layering with their own shirts. Let them paint designs on the front.

Accessorizing for Maximum Mileage

You can buy the simplest, well-made garments and give them a new look every time you wear them through your choice of accessories.

The possibilities are endless, but here are some ideas to start you thinking:

- Children's clothing needs little, if any, accessorizing. Accessory items just get in their way when they are playing. But book bags, hats, mittens, gloves, and scarves add interest and color. You will be replacing these items often because children lose them constantly. Don't spend much money on them.

- Dress up plain pumps with shoe clips.
- You can also use a shoe clip as a scarf holder. Just make sure the teeth on the clip will not damage the scarf.
- Watch closeout sales for textured, patterned hosiery. Buy decorative winter weights during summer when they are on sale. Winter will come again.
- Collect silk scarves. They can be used in many ways; one of the best is at the neckline.
- Get a booklet that tells how to tie scarves for maximum effect.
- Watch for sales on brightly colored, inexpensive costume jewelry. It adds interest and fun to your clothing.
- Men's clothing can be updated and brightened by adding a new shirt, and a new silk tie, and matching handkerchief.
- Shoes that are properly cared for help complete a man's wardrobe.
- A well-made umbrella or briefcase also helps add the finishing touch to a man's wardrobe.
- Men can add a vest or sweater for warmth and a different look.
- Don't forget your eyeglasses. They are an important accessory for both men and women. There is a trend toward having several pair of glasses for different occasions.
- Sunglasses are an important accessory too. Choose those that flatter your face. Avoid the reflective kinds that make you look like a grasshopper or a helicopter pilot flying into the sun.
- Keep your accessories simple, elegant, and orderly.
- Have a system for storing accessory items so that you don't have to search for the items when you are in a hurry.

Outlet Shopping

A true factory outlet is a room attached to the factory itself, like the Pendleton factory outlet in Washougel, Washington. There, in a portable building just across from the main entrance to the woolen factory, this famous company sells its goods at huge discounts. Some of the items are overruns on orders, some are seconds, but there often doesn't seem to be any reason why other garments are there. In addition to ready-made clothing, it is also possible to buy fabric, trim, buttons, and all the other sundries that go into making a Pendleton garment. If you can sew, you can make wonderful garments from Pendleton components at tremendous savings.

An outlet center is a great place for a family excursion.

This outlet is a lot different from the outlet centers found all over the country. True outlets tend to have better prices on their goods, because the factories are very eager to sell old stock. A true factory outlet is owned by the manufacturer and sells only goods made in its factories, although there may be many different labels on the goods.

At the Towle factory outlet in Massachusetts, I once bought silverplate for about one-fourth the retail cost. At other true outlets in that Massachusetts area, I bought skirts I'm still wearing after nine years, lingerie, and hosiery. All these purchases were made at tremendous savings.

I truly enjoy shopping at outlet centers. For one thing, everything I could possibly want to buy is in one place—everything from pots and pans to books, from designer clothes to toys. Besides that, there is usually a fun restaurant where you can get pizza by the slice, espresso, and marvelous desserts, among other wonderful edibles.

An outlet center is a great place for a family excursion. Besides being able to shop for everything you need and doing it together as a family, you can save from 30 to 70 percent.

If you are wondering where such outlets might be in your area, check the Internet. Check your local bookstore and even the chamber of commerce in your area or in any area you will be visiting. My first introduction to outlet shopping came when we stopped at an information booth at the Massachusetts state line and were handed an outlet guide. You will also find books in the library that are guides to factory outlets.

Here is some of the terminology that will help you be successful at outlet shopping:

Irregular—Items so marked will have slight imperfections that do not affect wearability.

Samples—Items made to show prospective buyers. They usually come in small sizes and often do not match other items in the designer's line.

As is—These are real markdown bargains, but be advised that there is always something wrong with these items. Check to find out what it is. It could be a broken zipper, soil, grease from manufacturing, or rips in the fabric itself. Find the flaw and decide if it is fixable or if it is a flaw you can live with for the price.

Discontinued—This means the line has been discontinued. You will not be able to replace or add to it later. This is probably more applicable to dishes and silverware than to clothing.

In addition to outlets, other kinds of stores where you may find bargains include:

Off-price stores that sell overruns and leftover goods from a variety of manufacturers rather than just one.

Discount stores that sell goods at a lower margin of profit than regular department stores.

Clearance centers that sell unsold seasonal goods from department store chains and other retailers.

To have the most success at shopping outlets, do the following:

✳ Make a list of what you need. The selection can be overwhelming once you reach the center.

✳ Go to local department stores and check out the prices of items you plan to buy for easy comparison.

✳ Find out about outlet store policies regarding credit cards, returns, and replacement of damaged goods.

✳ Remember the only true bargain is the one you need. No matter how great the saving, if you don't need it, you aren't saving anything.

✳ Check all clothing carefully for manufacturing defects. If you find them, ask for a higher discount.

✳ Get your name on the store's mailing list.

✳ Don't assume that the size marked in the garments is correct. Sometimes the reason the garment is in an outlet center is because it was improperly sized.

✳ Check the bins of mixed items. Items here may be dirty or in other ways shopworn and only need washing or minor repair to bring them up to quality.

✳ Think ahead. The clothing available in outlets may not be for the current season. Spring manufacturers' samples may come back for resale in the fall. If it is quality merchandise and of classic styling, it will still be in style next spring.

✳ Take children only if they will enjoy the excursion and only if they can endure a marathon shopping day. Most younger ones can't. Older children will enjoy the day most if the shopping is for them.

Thrifting

There is a way to save even more money than you can by shopping at outlets, discount, and close-out stores: Become a "junk store junkie." Shop at thrift and resale shops.

I am continually amazed at the amount and quality of goods that are thrown away in this country. Fortunately not all of it ends up in landfills right away. Sometimes several people have the opportunity to reuse an item before it is tossed for good.

I doubt if thrift store shopping would be as good in less prosperous countries of the world, but in this country, our affluence makes it possible for us to toss out items with scarcely a thought. Thrift store operation is big business, and usually thrift stores are crammed with bargain hunters.

Thrifting is not for everyone. Some people just can't stand the process of sorting through lots of unusable, broken stuff to find that one treasure. But if you can do it, you can save a lot.

I've made thrifting a game—a very profitable one, at that. The thrift shop where I go most often buys overruns and returned merchandise from one of the more prestigious store chains in America. This company is known for its return policy and customer service. They will exchange or take back goods with no questions asked. A lot of that superior merchandise finds its way to this thrift-shop chain, where I buy it for about one-third of its original cost.

The chain also buys closeouts of stores that are shutting down, overruns, and "as is" items from local factories, salesmen's samples, and other new (tagged) items.

When I knew I would be writing this book, I started saving tags from the items I bought at this thrift-shop chain and marking on the back what had been purchased. Let me give you some ideas of the clothing I have purchased and the savings I have realized.

A two-piece red cotton dress with lined skirt—$12.99. (I bought this outfit in the dead of winter.)

A navy blue leather purse—fully lined in leather—with a shoulder strap—$5.99.

A two-piece cotton knit Land's End dress—$6.99.

A red stitched-pleat skirt—$2.50. (This was on sale at half price. Even thrift stores have sales.)

A turquoise silk shell—$3.95.

A pink wool "Jones of New York" blazer—$4.50.

Once in a while I even spend more than $15.00 on an item. Here are some of those purchases.

A Guy Laroche red designer suit, fully lined and fully tailored—$19.99. For a dressy look, I added a cream-colored satin blouse inset with lace in a V shape. I purchased the blouse at an outlet in San Francisco for $35, rather than spending $75 or more in a department store.

A navy blue skimmer dress for summer—$24.95. The dress still had the manufacturer's tags in place. Two of the seven buttons were missing. Even if I had to replace all the buttons at $2.50 each, the dress was still a bargain.

A new peach-colored linen suit—$26. The only thing wrong with this suit was that the lining of one sleeve was twisted. I opened up the seam and resewed it in about fifteen minutes.

My thrifting adventures began many years ago. I discovered that thrift stores sold fabric pieces big enough to make garments for the children and for me as well. They also had a large assortment of buttons, zippers, thread, and all the other sewing notions needed—for pennies. So I started buying these items.

One day as I was on my way to the fabric area of the thrift store, I saw a little red coat with a black fur collar—size three. It was handmade, and had been exquisitely tailored. My mother had just given me a red velvet beret for my daughter. The coat's price was $3.50. I bought it, and she wore it for more than a year.

Later on when our son was due, I found a brand-new infant snowsuit for less than five dollars. It was then that I decided that if people were going to throw away wonderful items like these, I was going to find them and save money.

Because most children's clothing in this country is so well made and because children grow so quickly, there are lots and lots of clothes for them in thrift shops.

When buying children's clothing or anything else in a thrift store—or for that matter, anywhere—it's important to inspect it for damage. Stains and spots can be treated and often can be removed completely. Rit color remover is wonderful for removing stains on all white clothing and linens. Rips in seams, broken zippers, and missing buttons can all be fixed. Most tears in the fabric itself cannot be fixed inconspicuously, but maybe you can put an appliqué or trim over the tear. If you want a garment that has stains you're not sure will come out, consider the price and ask yourself if you can afford to throw it away if you fail to remove the stain. Or could you live with it, if the stain is permanent?

Resale Shops

A close cousin to thrift stores are resale or consignment shops. I buy little in consignment shops, for two reasons. I almost never find the new items I find in thrift stores, and the prices of the used goods are higher.

Resale shops are places where patrons sell used items, usually clothing, for a 50 percent split with the shop owner. Good shops have strict rules about the kind of merchandise they accept—usually good quality and it must be clean and pressed. There is often a time limit for selling the garment. If at the end of the allotted time no sale has been made, it is the patron's responsibility to claim it, or the shop owner will dispose of it.

Consignment and resale shops are big business where I live and probably in most areas of the country. Shops are listed in our local paper at least once a month in a group ad.

Each consignment and thrift store takes on a personality of its own. I'm not sure why that is, but I know that I go to one thrift shop if I'm looking for handbags. They seem always to have an abundance of them. I go to another place if I want to do it myself and sew, for this shop has lots of fabric. Then there are the shops that have new clothes, good belts, leather goods, and lots of silk scarves.

You learn which shops have more of which items by shopping them. I've found that if you go on a regular basis, you can determine what's new in a store in a few minutes and look at just those items. You don't have to look at everything every time. That would become overwhelming.

Shopping in Your Closet

Sometimes to have more clothes we just need a new way of looking at what we have in our closet. Try taking everything you own out of the closet and piling it on a bed. Then pick up each garment and evaluate it. Ask yourself the following questions:

Does it fit?
Does it flatter me?
Do I like this color?
Have I worn it this year?
Is there any reason why I should keep it?

If the answer to any of these questions is no, discard the garment. After going through the pile, take a look at the garments you have left. Try to determine why you like them, and keep this in mind for the next shopping trip.

Then try to look at your clothes in a new way. Look at your suits. Could the jacket of one suit be worn with a different skirt or pants? Could the skirt or pants be worn with several other shirts or blouses? Would a new scarf or tie give you a whole new look? Could you mix dressy and casual clothes for versatility? Could you cut off the top of a dress and turn the bottom into a skirt to wear with other shirts, sweaters, and blouses? Could you top a dated dress with a jacket or a cropped top, add jewelry, belts, or other accessory items, and bring it to life? Could you mix prints or color combinations you've never thought of before?

Sometimes buying one new item will give you dozens of new choices in your closet. For example, a good basic black, gray, or navy blue skirt or pants will mix with almost everything you own.

Try to look at your clothes in a new way.

I keep wearing the same black skirt with a number of jackets, sweaters, blouses, vests, and so forth. If I want a new outfit, I usually buy only the top and use the same old skirt. A black skirt is a black skirt is a black skirt; there's not much you can do to change it. I have a couple, in fact, in different lengths and fabric weights.

Anything multicolored gives you lots of mix-and-match options. A trendy multicolored sweater can be worn over almost everything you have.

Another device for shopping in your own wardrobe is organizing your closet so that you can find things. I use a system that is highly recommended by wardrobe planners: I group colors together. I hang all pants and skirts together in one place, but then they are hung by color families. I hang all blouses and all dresses in the same way. It's easy to find that certain blue blouse when you are organized this way.

Keep dressy clothes in a different place from the everyday wear. Put them at the back of the closet. Get some specialty hangers for belts and ties. Get as many as you need to do the job for you.

Perhaps one, two, or even several of the ideas in this chapter will help you find more dollars for family fun. Clothing is one of the big-ticket items for families today. If we buy into the myth that it costs a lot of money to look great, we will spend our dollars on clothing rather than on experiences that will enhance our family life together.

Maybe what's in this chapter will spark creative ideas for you as well. Don't stop with my ideas. Watch the supermarket magazines for money-saving tips on buying clothing.

18

Wheels

Several years ago, between buying Christmas gifts for my kids and buying milk, I decided to stop off at a local car dealership, just to see what they had. I had my heart set on a red Honda Prelude. Of course, I hoped I could get it with a full accessory package.

I began my conversation with the salesman by asking him about the car on the showroom floor. I quickly ascertained that I was not going to be able to afford the car. But as all good car salesmen do, he assured me that such cars keep their value and began to describe a used car that had come in earlier that day.

As I listened, I began to realize there was something he was not telling me. I said, "What color is that car?"

"Red," he answered.

"Is there some reason you're not showing it to me?" I asked.

"Well, it's on the back lot. Some people were looking at it."

"Did they put money down on it?" I asked.

"No."

"Can I see it?"

He took me out, and I slid behind the wheel of my dream car. It was four years old and had 25,000 miles on it, but I didn't care, because it was $9,000 cheaper than the new one on the floor and had everything I wanted—air-conditioning, sunroof, four-wheel steering, quadraphonic sound with equalizer. In fact I couldn't think of one more thing I would want to add.

"I suppose you want to drive it," he said.

"Yes, I sure do!" I told him.

I drove it, loved it, and then said to the salesman, "Is there any reason I can't buy it?"

"No," he said.

And so I bought it on the spot. Well, I made the down payment, and paid it off a couple of years later. The car has been everything I had ever hoped for and now has 150,000 miles on it (more later about keeping a car). Up until then, I had driven the family "junk car." I was thrilled to have my own dream car.

I'm not unusual. We Americans continue our love affair with the automobile, despite the fact that they cost more than we could ever have imagined a few years back, despite the fact that gasoline and repair costs keep escalating, and despite the fact that insurance costs are out of sight.

An automobile is the second most expensive item in the family budget, the first being a house. Because a car seems to be the extension of many people's personality, and because the purchase of a car is a highly emotional experience, we tend to forget some of our financial skills, throw caution to the wind, and buy what we love. Then later on we suffer the consequences of our actions. Sometimes we find we've spent too much for the car or we haven't bought a car that meets our family's needs. By the time we realize our mistake, the car has already begun to depreciate. To avoid these problems, we have to think and plan ahead.

It's wise to save for a car and pay cash. By paying cash you will realize a major savings on interest payments. I didn't follow my own advice and I realize now that one or two month's car payments are for interest. That's a lot of money to give away.

Ron Blue says, in his book *A Woman's Guide to Financial Peace of Mind,* "If you can't afford to save for a car, you can't afford to borrow for it, either. If you believe this, it means you will drive the car you now own a little longer, or wait a little longer to purchase a first car."[9]

Do You Need a Car?

Of course, you need a car! Is there any question about it? The question should be asked. The best way to save money on car expenses is to not own a car. Most of us truly do need a car, but there are some of us who could do without one. Those who have figured out a way to do without a car manage quite well. They don't need car payments, insurance payments, gas fill-ups, and all the rest.

If you live in a city with a good transit system, it may well be that you can use it to get everywhere you need to go. In some cities a car is actually a liability. If you live in an apartment or condominium, you need a place to park your car. Sometimes apartment complexes have parking; sometimes they don't. Often the only parking spot is outdoors or perhaps even on the street, where the car is subject to all kinds of damage.

If you live in a city and drive to work, you have to navigate the traffic, deal with the fact that you are contributing to pollution, and find a place to park at work. In some cities, places to park are almost nonexistent or so expensive that you may feel you are making a daily investment in urban real estate.

If you choose to commute by public transit, what do you do about those times when you truly need a car? Splurge and call a cab or a limo. It's cheaper than paying car-related expenses. Rent a car for a trip or vacation. What could be nicer than taking a family trip in a brand-new car? Weekly rates for rental cars are fairly low, compared to the cost of owning a car.

But even when all the logic is understood, most of us will still want to own a car for the flexibility, independence, and mobility it gives our family. In that case, maybe we should think about the possibility of owning less car. Think about buying a good, small used car and paying cash for it. Perhaps it would be all you need for errands and short family trips. Maybe commuting could be done by public transportation and your family could rent a full-size car for that once-a-year vacation.

Think it through and don't buy more car than you need to provide adequate transportation for your family.

How Many Cars Do You Need?

Only in an affluent country like the United States would anyone think to ask how many cars you need. In most countries of the world, there is no question about owning even one car, but here we wonder how many cars we should have.

The answer to the question is easy: Don't own more cars than you need. Once we lived in the suburbs of a city that had no public transportation, and we had only one car. I usually had to walk where I wanted to go, or wait until evening to use the family car. Fortunately we weren't too far from a grocery store, so it was possible to walk there and bring home a few groceries.

But it wasn't easy to be without a car. Once I walked two miles to a bus stop. That took about forty minutes. Then I waited another forty minutes in the cold for the bus, which was running late. I boarded the bus only to find that it stopped at almost every street corner. What would have been a twenty-minute car trip turned into a half-day event.

So there definitely are times when owning a second car makes life easier. But what should that second car be? Take a look at your lifestyle. Do you need a station wagon to transport the ball team? Do you need a small pickup to haul yard debris or furniture? Do you need a small car for running errands? Is your family filled with sports enthusiasts who need to tow or top-carry boats, skis, bicycles, or other gear? Or are you, like me, thinking about the need for a four-wheel sports vehicle to get through the snow?

Think about the interests and activities of your family and buy only what you need. That need may change as time goes on. You may have wanted to pull a trailer at one point in your life and later on decided to stay in hotels. You may have lived where you needed a snow-friendly automobile, and now you've moved to the desert. Life changes; needs change. So if you see that you now own more car than you need, sell it and buy less.

Buying the First Family Car

I like buying new cars. I like shopping for different models, doing the research to determine which car uses the least gasoline per mile, investigating which cars need the least repairs and how expensive those repairs will be when they are needed. I like determining how big an engine is needed and what accessory items are essential and which would only be wonderful to have. I want to know what the resale value is on a particular model.

Whenever possible, buy a new car for the number-one family car. Dependability is important in a family automobile, so if you are going to have a car for your family, buy the best you can afford.

When buying a new car for a family, it is important to think about the upholstery. Although none of us would complain about real leather or plush seats, try to think what they will look like after Suzy mashes a cookie into the upholstery. Children are messy, in case you haven't noticed. They spill things, chew things, track all kinds of unmentionables into a car, and can even get sick in a car. Perhaps for a family, good old vinyl seats are the best investment.

Someone in the family needs to do research on different kinds of cars. Research can be done through reading automotive magazines and *Consumer Report,* talking with dealers of various kinds of cars, and talking with people who are satisfied with the car model they have chosen.

One of the reasons I wanted the car I bought was that I had done all the research and found it met all of my criteria. I also had a friend who had an identical car and loved it. After eleven years I am still satisfied with the car, and I hope it never wears out; but if it does, I hope I can buy another just like it. Now that's satisfaction!

How to Shop for a Car

The way to shop for a car is probably not the way I did it— dropping into a dealership between the Christmas gifts and the milk and buying a car. A better way is to visit several showrooms, talk to the salesmen (who will be only too happy to talk with you), look at the various models, test drive several kinds of cars, do your research, and then make your decision.

The whole business of test driving a car is very important. Take the car for as long as the dealer will allow. A car may seem comfortable to drive and ride in for the first half-hour, but after that, it may become increasingly uncomfortable. A compact economy car is not a good buy if you are miserable the whole time you are riding in it.

Everyone in the family who will be driving the car should come along. Let them evaluate the maneuverability, handling, ride, visibility, ventilation, and whether the gauges and controls are easy to use. Take the car on the freeway to check for interior noise. See if the car has enough acceleration power to pass slower vehicles easily. How does the car handle on curves and in traffic? When a passenger is comfortably seated in the front seat, is there room for someone to sit in the back? What happens when the little people in your family grow to be big people? Will there still be room for their legs? Will there be headroom for them and everyone else? What will it be like to load and unload cargo from this car? Will there even be room for cargo, or will you have to attach a top carrier, which will seriously increase gas consumption?

Ron Blue tells how he taught his daughter Cynthia to buy a car. First, he had her visit several dealerships to determine what features she wanted in a car. Then Ron and Cynthia went back to the dealerships together, to determine what the initial offer from the dealers would be. Then they began bargaining. They asked salesman number one for the best price he could give them, then went to salesman number two and asked him. They visited several dealerships and got their best price. Then they went back to all of the previous salesmen and told them the best price they had been offered. In every case, the salesmen lowered their price, until eventually no one would lower the price any further. Cynthia finally paid about 15 percent below the sticker price.[10]

Getting the Money to Buy a Car

Coming up with the money for a car is not as big a problem as it should be. Car loans are relatively easy to get. Dealers don't seem to care if you put a huge down payment on the car or if you finance every dollar, but *you* should care.

Put the biggest down payment you can afford on the car and try to repay the loan in the shortest time you can. This will probably make your monthly payment quite large, but you will save substantially on interest charges.

Some dealerships have package deals for loans whereby you finance the car through their own finance company and get your insurance at the same place. Package deals are usually not such great deals. Shop separately for financing and insurance.

Talk to your own banker—the one you've established credit with over the years. Your own bank wants to keep you as a customer and will therefore do their best for you. Their advice about your car loan will also be given from the standpoint of a long-term relationship with you, their customer.

How Long Should You Keep the Car?

Many people buy a new car every two or three years. They feel it helps them keep up with the depreciation factor. But others like to keep their cars longer, pay them off, and have a small respite from car payments. Remember that if you are saving for a new car, you are also accumulating interest on the money you are putting in the bank. Ron Blue says, "If you take out a loan to buy a car like most people—you'll be on the wrong side of the magic of compounding. Instead of earning interest on your savings, the bank will be earning interest on your payments. Lenders know this, which is why they're so ready to loan you money."[11]

Ron also says, "Research shows that absolutely the cheapest car you will ever drive is the car you presently own. The cost of replacement and the incidental costs of a new car far outweigh the repair and maintenance costs of an older car. It's never advantageous from a purely economic standpoint to replace your car."[12]

Studies have compared the cost of buying a new car every one or two years with the cost of keeping a car for a decade. Look for this information in the popular money books that are available.

If you decide to drive your car longer than a couple of years, regular servicing of the vehicle is very important. Perhaps nothing extends the life of a car more than regular oil and filter changes. It may seem like an unnecessary expense, and you may be tempted to forget it, but this is an expense that avoids many problems with your automobile. Other servicing, such as regular lubrication, emission adjustments, and air filter changes, also help extend the life of a car.

If resale is important to you (and it should be), then it is important to take care of the finish and interior of the car. No one likes to buy a dirty used car, unless it is very cheap.

Alternate Forms of Transportation

There are many modes of transportation other than automobiles. Motorcycles, bicycles, and mopeds can all be used as transportation. Many cities have made or are in the process of making bike lanes to safely accommodate bicycle traffic. Biking is an economical means of transportation, and after a few miles of commuting by bicycle, one does not have to be concerned about additional aerobic exercise. Think about it. Nonmotorized biking does not pollute the atmosphere, provides aerobic exercise, is inexpensive, does not contribute to traffic congestion, and it can sometimes be quicker than a car in traffic.

As with everything, there is an upside and a downside to using a bike for transportation. What does one wear to bike to work? If there is a place to change at the office, you can wear regular biking clothes. Of course, that means taking a change of clothes with you, and that can be a problem too. If there is no place to change, you'll have to work all day in the clothes you biked to work in.

Where do you put your bike when you get to work? Some people remove the front wheel and chain it and the entire bike to a post. Some offices allow bikes in a storage area or in an out-of-the-way hallway. This is something companies that are concerned about the environment need to think about.

If you can find a way to commute to work by bicycle, it can be a great saving of money. If you can't, perhaps you can encourage your children to ride their bikes more.

Studies that show how little exercise our children are getting these days are frightening. Children need to be encouraged to be outdoors, playing, exercising, and even working. One of the ways they can do this is by riding their bikes to and from activities.

It is also frightening to learn how many young people are crippled for life by head injuries. Bicycle, moped, and motorcycle riders must wear helmets. When you buy your child her first bike, also buy a helmet and insist she wear it at all times. That helmet may be the most important piece of equipment you ever buy your child.

Another wise investment is a bicycle safety course. Often these are provided by schools, local police or traffic officers, or by city park and recreation departments. Children must know the rules of the road to be safe. They must know the safe roads where they can ride and those roads that are unsafe.

Since biking is such great exercise and recreation for the entire family, think about investing in bikes for everyone, then teach your child about safe biking by going with her and setting a good example.

Finding Inexpensive Bicycles

Speaking about bicycles and saving money, let's talk about where we can find bicycles at a good price.

First of all, the same rules apply here as they do to a car: Don't buy more bike than you need. Think about how you will be using your bike—for short hops to the store, riding to school or work, or going on cross-country trips. This will help you determine the type of bike and how many gears you need. Talk to bike shop salesmen and read biking magazines to get the best advice.

Secondhand bikes that fit your needs may be available. They are sold at garage sales, through newspaper ads, or in thrift and secondhand shops. Bikes are something children eventually outgrow, and everyone has to dispose of them. Since bikes are basic, old bikes can be revived by the purchase of new tires, a good servicing at a bike shop, some scrubbing, and perhaps some paint.

Watch for local police auctions. Police pick up abandoned and stolen bikes on a regular basis. Once or twice a year, they will hold an auction and sell off these unclaimed bikes. You can purchase a really great bike for a minuscule price.

Mopeds and Motorcycles

Mopeds and motorcycles are in an entirely different league than bicycles. I have known people who think motorcycle travel is the most exciting travel in the world. I have met couples in campgrounds traveling double on a motorcycle, pulling a little trailer with all their camping gear. They go thousands of miles and love the feel of the wind in their faces, the economy of this means of travel, and the complete freedom they experience when traveling by bike. These are ordinary people—businessmen and women, homemakers and executives, parents and kids. Although I am not an aficionado of the motorcycle, it bears looking into for some families.

We seem destined to have wheels under us, and since we are, it is wise to give serious thought to cost, safety, convenience, and wise environmental consumerism.

19

Get it Free or Get it Cheap

A few years ago I went to a concert given by one of the best bands in the country, the United States Air Force band. They played a little patriotic music, a little movie theme music, a little Dixieland jazz, and a little big-band music. It was wonderful, and the price was right—it was free.

Every community has some free musical events.

Free Musical Events

Most big city orchestras give free concerts at various times during the year. You will also find free musical performances at local colleges. Music students are required to give performances for their degree. Their recitals are free and they need an audience. Their music, while quite structured, is well rehearsed. It has to be, if they are going to graduate. Music faculty often give free recitals as well.

There are all kinds of other free musical events. Some restaurants feature a musician. I can think of a favorite restaurant where a truly superb pianist plays every Saturday morning. The place is packed. And at another restaurant a guitarist plays classical guitar.

Free Theater

Free theater may be a bit more difficult to find than free music, but in many cities around the country there are theater-in-the-park programs that are free. Not free, but very inexpensive, are the dramatic presentations of high schools, colleges, and local theater groups.

Of course, the ultimate free fun with the theater is to get involved in it yourself. I know a family with four children, now almost grown, who have from time to time all been involved in productions, sometimes individually and sometimes as a family. Think of the fun it must be for the whole family to be in a play together.

All the members of your family may not be actors, but they could be involved in other parts of the production: creating sets, making costumes, stage managing, and lighting.

Swapping

Swapping (not swap meets) has almost become a lost art. Maybe it's because we tend to live in splendid isolation. Maybe it's because we all have so much money we can just toss out the things our money has bought. But swapping is still a wonderful way to save money.

What do you have that I could use? What do I have that you need? Perhaps one of the most obvious things to swap is children's clothing. Most clothing can be worn by several children, especially by two- or three-year-olds, who grow too fast to wear it out.

Children's clothing, children's furniture, and children's toys are all well made, and the need for them quickly passes. These are good items to swap with other families.

Some churches set up places where swapping can take place. Instead of having a garage sale, why not have a neighborhood swap meet, when goods are exchanged, not money? Swap housework, expertise, houseplant cuttings, driving the kids to school, baby-sitting.

Swapping can be arranged informally (talking with a neighbor over the back fence) or formally (putting an ad in the paper).

There is, in most papers, a column for just this. This column is fun to read. I've never found anything I wanted to swap, but I might someday.

The Neighbors' Throwaways

What are the neighbors throwing out? Don't laugh, and don't cringe. People throw away tons of good items every year. Most of them feel guilty about what they are throwing away and would be relieved if someone would take it off their hands.

It seems that people who live in apartment complexes are especially quick to throw away useful and often new items. I suppose this is because they move often and are constantly unburdening themselves of extra possessions.

People throw good things away because it's easier than finding someone to give them to. Keep your eyes open for items you can use that your neighbors are tossing out.

Free Animals

Almost every day the newspaper carries ads offering animals for free. I have seen ads for nearly every kind of purebred dog imaginable, offered for free because an owner was moving somewhere the pet would not be welcome.

Before investing in an expensive puppy from a store in a mall, see if you can find one for free. Or check the local humane society. The only fees you'll pay are for shots and spaying or neutering. In some cases there are no fees at all, just a suggested contribution.

If you tell the humane society people what you are looking for and are patient, you will probably get what you want eventually. Our beautiful blonde cocker spaniel came from the pound. She had just been groomed and was as pretty as any dog you've ever seen. She was a great pet.

I'm sure you know that kittens are easy to adopt without a dime. It's also possible to obtain rabbits, birds, and many other species without spending a cent. In fact if you have the space, it is possible to get wild mustangs from several places in the country. These wild horses are overpopulating and threatening rangeland. The government periodically rounds them up and offers them to whomever can care for them.

Or you may want to adopt a greyhound. When greyhounds that are used for racing have lost their speed, they are killed. There are now organizations that try to find homes for these wonderful, gentle animals, so they won't be euthanized.

So before you rush off to a pet store, think about other alternatives for obtaining a pet. If you can get an animal that is right for your family for free, you have saved a lot of money.

The Public Library

One of the best sources of free services is the public library. I am continually amazed at what libraries offer today, in addition to books.

If you haven't been to a library lately, go this week. Of course, you'll find books, and also records, CDs, cassettes, videos, magazines, artwork, pamphlets on every subject you can think of, free information, and free services. Most offer computer terminals with Internet access as well.

Years ago, when our children were small and we had very little money, I discovered that you can check out an art print from the library and have it in your home for a number of weeks. I had a couple of places in the house where there was a wall hook for hanging framed prints from the library. We had some unusual prints over the years. See what your library offers in the way of artwork.

The local library is also a great source of information about many subjects. One town library conducted master gardener sessions. A master gardener would come in about once a month and answer questions on gardening. Other programs focus on taxes, crime prevention, decorative arts, pet care, and a lot more. A great attempt is being made in many cities to make the library a user-friendly place.

Another source of information in many libraries is an information line. You can call and ask the most obtuse question and usually get an answer.

When writing my last book, I had put a quote in the book that I picked up from some secondary source. The publisher questioned the exact source of the quote, and it was my task to find out where it had come from. I called the library information line and asked them. Within a half hour, I had my answer and more information than I could possibly use. All I did was pick up the phone and call.

I have also found when researching a topic that most librarians love to get involved. They find sources and books that I never thought of and they act as if it is the most important thing they have to do that day.

Tax information is available at the library. All of the needed tax forms are there at tax time. There are recommended books on taxes available for checkout. At our local library there is an information sheet that tells when local tax offices are open and where they are located. There is a listing of toll-free numbers for patrons to call for help with taxes. There is a volunteer income-tax assistance program held right in the library facilities. And to go the extra mile, the library remains open until midnight on April 15. That evening there is a representative from the U.S. Postal Service available at a drive-up window to collect the completed tax forms. There is a representative from the state revenue office who answers questions, volunteers are available in force, and there is even a stamp machine with a bill changer available. How's that for service?

Another wonderful feature our local library offers is database information. You pay a two dollar surcharge and eleven dollars per hour online. A trained library searcher can recommend the databases that are most appropriate for the information you need. The library also provides lists of databases available in your area.

To keep costs to a minimum, the library staff searcher can perform an initial online search that results in a printout of bibliographic references. These can be used to get the full text of a document from the library.

You can tell the searcher how much you can afford, and he or she will help you get the most information possible for the least amount of money.

Our local library also has a database called Maggie's Place. When you log onto this database, this is the kind of information available:

1. Public access catalog—a listing of all the library district's book, video, audio, and CD collections.
2. A collection of databases—social and community agencies, community calendar, child care sources, clubs, education opportunities, local authors, senior housing options, arts, and much more.
3. Encyclopedia and other references.
4. Local government databases that provide information about all local and civic activities.
5. Menus of other library systems.

The library also sponsors a Great Books Discussion Group of adults interested in reading and discussing great literary works. The groups have from ten to twenty people in them. The choice of material for discussion is classical literature such as *The Federalist* by Hamilton, Jay, and Madison, and *The City of God* by Saint Augustine. It is free except for the materials that you must purchase and read.

Many libraries have a bookmobile system, making it possible to check out books at many different locations throughout the city.

For children there are story times, summer reading programs, and film festivals.

Free Sporting Events

Most families are all too aware of the free opportunities their children have for participation in all kinds of team sports. There is Little League baseball, football, field hockey, and in some places the strangest sport of all—rugby. (I've watched rugby games and never could figure out what the purpose was supposed to be, unless you count seeing how dirty you can get.)

There are plenty of participatory sports activities for children that are free. But what about those professional games that are so expensive? Most professional teams offer free tickets to organizations, and there are even free days. Get a schedule from a team near you or in a city you will be visiting, and find out what they are offering and when.

if Not Free, Then Cheap

Swap Meets

For some people, swap meets or flea markets may be going too far in the money-saving business. Swap meets are usually held in a field or near an auction barn on a Saturday or Sunday. Those with goods to sell rent a space, back their vehicles (of all kinds and conditions) into a space, open the trunk, and spread out their goods, sometimes on tables and sometimes on the ground.

Buyers walk up and down the rows, looking at all this stuff, from cheap plastic toys to old pieces of furniture. You can buy fabric, baseball cards, old and new tools, rugs, handicrafts, old and new china—truly almost anything you can think of.

Recently, for fun, I went to a swap meet on a Saturday afternoon. The one thing I found that interested me (but not enough to buy it) was a serger for sewing. It was at a very reasonable price and looked in great condition. I asked the seller about the equipment. He said he had purchased it from a store that had gone bankrupt. It was brand new.

What's swapped most at swap meets is conversation. People stand around talking to each other, and they are willing to talk with you. It is a lot of fun.

There are people who follow the swap-meet circuit and make a living selling at them. Watch these people pack and unpack. They have it down to a science. Then there are people from your community who have cleaned out their garage and want to sell the excess. Swap meets are like gigantic garage sales.

Perhaps the most interesting swap meet I've ever been to is held in Shipshawana, Indiana. This is in the heart of the Amish country, and the Amish people bring their wonderful handcrafted items to sell. It is possible to buy handmade quilts, lace, knit goods, handcrafted furniture, and unbelievably delicious food products. There is an air of stepping back a century to a simpler time when the county fair was the biggest event of the year.

Garage Sales

Garage sales are fun to have and to attend. They're a good way to rid yourself of excess stuff, if you don't mind setting up and running the sale.

I know a couple that has traveled to Europe several times in the last few years. They've acquired the funds to travel by buying pieces of furniture at garage sales, fixing them up, and reselling them at their own garage sale.

Once when they were visiting, we made the rounds of garage sales. One of the things my friend bought was a golf bag that had several clubs in it but not a complete set. At home he had several other clubs and he planned to build a complete set, which he would then sell for a good price. Because I was out with them, I ended up buying a brand-new four-man rubber raft for seventeen dollars.

Another time I went to a garage sale with my brother. He bought a Stanley wood plane for twenty-five cents. It had been lying in the corner of someone's garage for a number of years and was very dirty and rusty. Within fifteen minutes of getting it home, he had it cleaned up like new. Since his hobby is restoring wooden boats, he was delighted to have another plane.

Perhaps the delight of thrift shopping is the serendipity of it all. You just never know what you will find next. Often the item you find may not be of great value, unless you need it and get it for much less than you would pay at a department store, in which case it has great value to you. You can save money on that item and use the money you save for a family outing.

As has been so aptly said, "One man's trash is another man's treasure." If you don't believe that statement, have your own garage sale and put a price on the stuff you are sure no one would ever want. Watch what happens. My experience in garage sales is limited, because I would rather give things away than set up and tend a garage sale. But once I did have a sale and I put together several boxes of items that I thought truly belonged in the trash can. A friend said, "Try to sell it. You can always throw it away later. I think you'll be surprised what they'll buy." I think I put a price of one dollar on each box. Those boxes were among the first to go.

Although you can buy anything at a garage sale, some of the best buys are in furniture, appliances, children's clothing, sporting equipment and games, collector's items such as baseball cards and china, camping gear, and automotive products such as tires and carrying racks.

Clothing for adults is usually dated or worn, and household linens are usually nearly worn out. Unless you are buying these items for rags or knock-about clothing, they aren't good buys.

Money-Saving Ideas for Travel

There are thousands of ideas for money-saving travel. Here is a potpourri of them:

1. Stop at state welcoming centers and pick up brochures that tell you where the best bargains are to be found in recreational ideas, places to stay, and even places for bargain shopping.

2. When making reservations, always ask for the best discounts.

3. Investigate traveling by train and bus. A train trip could be a great adventure for your kids.

4. Eat out in the best restaurants, but do it for breakfast or lunch. These meals are less expensive.

5. Limit your eating out in restaurants and plan it into your budget.

6. Some theme parks have reduced (twilight) fares later in the day.

7. In a large city you can sometimes rent a furnished apartment for a week. This is considerably less expensive than paying big-city hotel rates.

8. Investigate bed and breakfast inns. There are books that list B&Bs all across the country. Make sure kids are welcome. Remember, breakfast comes with the price of the room.

9. Investigate hotel chains that let kids stay in their parents' room free. Book early.

10. Go to the zoo. Most are either free or very inexpensive. Even if the zoo charges an admission fee, it may have a free day.

11. Visit art galleries and other museums. They are either inexpensive or free.

12. Visit factories that have free tours. Make arrangements ahead of time.

13. Visit state capitol buildings. They are often filled with history, and there is usually a guided tour.

14. Visit historic cities such as Williamsburg, Jamestown, or Yorktown, Virginia. Get out and walk through these wonderful old restored areas.

15. For other city walk ideas, check out Frommer's city guide books.

I believe there is a way to beat the high cost of living. I believe it takes some concentration, some attention to what's available, and some effort to find those hidden bargains. For some people, it will take a change of mind-set. The local thrift shop is not Saks or Nordstroms.

What I like to do is save all the money I can on everything possible, so that once in a while I can go to a department store and buy something I've wanted for a long time. I visit these stores with regularity, whether I buy or not. It is a wonderful way of improving my taste, staying knowledgeable about what is available, and being able to recognize brand names and the most up-to-date styles when I find them other places.

Another inexpensive way of keeping abreast of changing styles, changing trends in home decorating, changing ideas, and changing automobile design and development is to read magazines. I usually pick up a *Vogue* pattern magazine as soon as it hits the newsstand. *Vogue* styles run almost two years ahead of retail stores, so I know what's coming into fashion long before it hits the stores. Popular home magazines give you lots of ideas and tips for decorating and fixing up your home. Many magazines tell you how to do it yourself and save money.

There are two ways, at least, to approach this whole business of saving money when you shop. One is to feel sorry for yourself that you don't have enough money to go to the finest stores and shop. The other—the one I recommend—is to see it all as a great adventure. You never know what treasure you'll find next. You can enjoy the purchase because it didn't cost an arm and a leg. You can use it because you don't have your life savings tied up in that one item. You can get rid of it when you're finished with it for the same reason. And once in a while, you can take your family someplace truly special, without financial stress and without guilt, because you've been thrifty with your money and you've saved for this event.

If you learn to spend wisely throughout the year, you will have the necessary funds to enjoy day-to-day family fun, yearly vacations, and a sane, fiscally sound life.

20

30 Family Fun Adventures for Little or No Money

Many family adventures require little or no money but they are great fun and provide what is most important—time for a family to be together and enjoy each other. Here are some ideas you may want to try.

1. Give your children a limited amount of money and take them to a swap meet, thrift store, or garage sale. Challenge them to see how many treasures they can get for their money.

2. Take a hike and see what nature will provide for craft projects. Look for interesting branches, mosses, leaves, flowers, stones, pods, and so forth. When you get home, help the children make something with their treasures.

3. Make sock puppets by putting a rubber band around the toe of a sock. Decorate the sock with eyes, glasses, teeth, lips, and so forth. Peel-off labeling material is excellent for making the puppet's features. Show your children how to put their hand inside and make the puppet talk. Have a puppet show, using one of their favorite stories and their homemade puppets.

4. Take a walk through a garden or an area where flowers are grown for seeds or bulbs. Perhaps you'll see, as we once

did, a whole hillside covered with iris, or miles and miles of tulips forming a huge patchwork, or a garden where exotic and wonderful roses abound. Have the children vote on the most beautiful flower they see.

5. Attend ethnic food-tasting events. In our area, communities frequently have food fairs where all kinds of wonderful treats are available. The cost is minimal.

6. Take a ferryboat ride. Have a meal aboard the ferry; watch for aquatic life; look at the city's skyline from this very different viewpoint.

7. Go to the top of a tall building that has an observation deck. Help the children identify familiar landmarks from this height. Give a prize to the one who gets the most right.

8. Hang a sheet across a doorway and have a shadow play. Put a light on the actors' side to project their shadows onto the sheet. A fun thing to do is pretend to perform surgery, removing various items from "the patient"—the more absurd the item, the funnier.

9. Arrange a tour of a printing plant and see the high-speed equipment in action.

10. Go to a fish hatchery to see fingerlings or migrating fish.

11. Set goals for family cleanup chores. Who can clean his or her room the fastest? How long did it take to clean up after dinner last night? Can we better that time today?

12. Teach a child a craft—knitting, crocheting, simple wood-crafting, or gardening. This will enable the child to produce his own presents for Christmas and birthdays.

13. Help children make their own wrapping paper by block printing plain paper or paper bags with fruits and vegetables cut in half. Potatoes can be carved into shapes; lemons and oranges make an interesting print; half of an apple will work too.

14. Encourage older children to have a garage sale. They should plan the day, do the advertising, collect the goods, mark the items, and plan what to do with unsold items. They should be allowed to keep any profits.

15. Let the children play store with your canned goods, using a muffin tin as a cash drawer. Provide small change or

play money, and help them learn to make change and purchase wisely.

16. Let little kids play in the kitchen sink with soap bubbles, an egg beater, and other cooking implements. When they're finished, simply wipe up.

17. Spend time together looking at old family photos and telling the children what was happening when those photos were taken.

18. Organize a neighborhood basketball tournament at someone's house, a school, or playground.

19. Collect bugs and identify them by using a book from the library.

20. Plant grapefruit, lemon, orange, or apple seeds. If they are not a hybrid variety they will sprout. Suspend an avocado seed in water by inserting toothpicks in the sides to hold it in place. Do the same with various kinds of potatoes.

21. Check out videos from your library for an evening of video fun.

22. Go sledding or tubing with the family.

23. Have a family walkathon. Each person should select a walking-distance goal according to his or her age. Post these on a chart by week or month. Have family members record their daily walking distances.

24. Play an old-fashioned game with your kids like kick the can or hide and seek. They'll love it.

25. Mix up a batch of salt dough and keep it in the refrigerator for impromptu projects.

26. Make a calendar for Grandma and Grandpa by drawing twelve pictures and gluing them on another calendar. Or make twelve copies of a page with a grid at the bottom for the dates and blank at the top for the children's pictures. Help the kids fill in the dates.

27. Get a big box from an appliance store and give it to the kids. Watch their imaginations take over.

28. Begin a family history by interviewing family members. Using a cassette recorder, have them tell stories. Sometimes it helps older family members who might be intim-

idated by a tape recorder to be interviewed with a group. As one begins to talk, others add their viewpoints to the story. These tapes will be treasured in years to come when family members have died.

29. Buy disposable cameras for your children and let them take pictures of anything they choose. After the photos have been developed, talk about techniques that will produce better photos next time. The children can put their favorites in their own inexpensive album.

30. As a family, design a board game and draw it on a piece of poster board. Find small objects around the house for game pieces or use pieces from old games. Decide on the rules and write them down. Then play the game and see how it works.

Notes

Chapter 9 *Looking for Time*

1. Alan Lakein, *How to Get Control of Your Time and Life* (New York: New American Library, 1970).
2. Eugenia Price, *Leave Yourself Alone* (Grand Rapids: Zondervan, 1979).
3. Pat King, *How to Have All the Time You Need Every Day* (Wheaton: Tyndale House, 1980), 22.

Chapter 13 *Beg, Buy, or Barter Time*

4. Charlene Canape, *The Part-time Solution* (New York: Harper and Row, 1990), 2.
5. Gwen Ellis, *101 Ways to Make Money at Home* (Ann Arbor, Mich.: Servant, 1996).

Part 3 *Finding Dollars for Family Fun*

6. Larry Burkett, *Using Your Money Wisely* (Chicago: Moody, 1985), 18.

Chapter 15 *Su Casa, Mi Casa*

7. For more decorating ideas, see Gwen Ellis and Jo Ann Janssen, *Decorating on a Shoe-string* (Nashville, Tenn.: Broadman and Holman, 1999).
8. For more budget ideas, see Gwen Ellis and Jo Ann Janssen, *Decorating on a Shoestring*.

Chapter 18 *Wheels*

9. Ron Blue, *A Woman's Guide to Financial Peace of Mind* (Colorado Springs: Focus on the Family, 1991), 62.
10. Ibid., 63.
11. Ibid., 62.
12. Ibid.